What Autism Gave Me

A Devastating Diagnosis To A Triumphant Life

MICHAEL HAIGWOOD GOODROE

outskirts
press

Outskirts Press, Inc.
http://www.outskirtspress.com

Paperback ISBN: 978-1-4787-9782-1
Hardback ISBN: 978-1-4787-9788-3

PRINTED IN THE UNITED STATES OF AMERICA

Table of Contents

Giving Autism a Voice

I WAS THRILLED to learn that a memoir was being written about Michael's life experiences. I met Michael and his mother, Joane, several years ago when they came for Michael to serve on a panel at our regional Autism Conference at Jacksonville State University. After conversations with Michael and Joane following the conference that year, I knew that Michael should be our keynote speaker for the next year's conference. We always try to have a person on the autism spectrum or a parent of a person on the autism spectrum as our keynote speaker. I was so intrigued by Michael's story of success. He had overcome so many obstacles common to this disorder and he had risen above those challenges to not only attain a degree, but was also able to go on to graduate school to attain an MBA. Michael is also a second-degree black belt in Taido karate, a gifted singer, and comic book writer.

I teach in the Special Education Program in the School of Education at Jacksonville State University. I am also the assistant director for the Center for Autism Studies at the University. I have over twenty years in the field of special education and I have served as a classroom teacher, central office specialist and instructor at the university level. I also have a nephew on the autism spectrum. I have had special interest and developed expertise in the field of autism spectrum disorder (ASD) in the last fifteen years.

In my experience, I have found that so many young people diagnosed with autism spectrum disorder allow this label to limit them. This is why it is essential that we promote success stories like Michael's. It is so common for young people that had the same bleak prognosis early in life to allow this to dominate and incapacitate their vision for their life. Many of these students possess unique talents in areas of math, science, writing, and music. But most have chosen to discontinue their education after high school. Because of this, they are either employed making minimum wage at menial task jobs that are considerably below their personal capabilities, or they are collecting disability checks and staying home to play video games rather than being productive members of society. We are failing them. I believe this is all too often the scenario because we fail to empower them to reach their full potential in life.

It is critical that we raise the collective awareness and understanding of the general population about this disorder. We must change the paradigm to create an environment for growth and ultimately success for persons with ASD by focusing on their unique talents and abilities rather than focusing on their disability. I believe that this story is a great model for how we can accomplish this task.

Michael had the necessary support along the way to facilitate his current level of success. And his parents made sure that this happened for him. They never allowed him to limit himself. There is speculation that Albert Einstein possibly had high-functioning autism. If he had lived at a time that this diagnosis was more recognized and prevalent such as our current climate, what might have happened in his life? Is it possible that we might not have his contributions to math and science? Would we even have the Theory of Relativity? These are thought-provoking questions that we must ask ourselves.

This has the potential to become a major crisis in our society if we do not do more to promote success in the lives of persons with ASD. Our current prevalence rate, according to the Centers for Disease Control, is 1 in 68 children. Those children will grow up. What are we going to do to address this? It is certainly a problem if we do not develop a plan for assisting in their transition to adulthood. Michael's story is not only inspirational, but it can be used as a guide for parents and educators alike to address this crisis with proactive measures.

Now, back to Michael and his personal experience. I have to admit when Michael came to speak, I was a little nervous at first, as I had never heard him present to an audience and I wasn't quite sure how he would perform. I can tell you the audience was completely mesmerized within the first five minutes of his presentation. Michael's story is one of hope and inspiration. He received a standing ovation at the conclusion of his presentation; people were lined up to meet him and speak with him. It was a very powerful presentation and his is a very powerful story.

After Michael's presentation, I encouraged him to write a book. I am so thankful that he took that advice to heart. He has a voice that will not be silenced. A voice that delivers hope.

--Valerie Whitehead Wheat,
Center for Autism Studies,
Jacksonville State University

Introduction to the Unimaginable

FOR THE CHILD whose life was once characterized as limited, Michael has an unexpected story of hope to tell. His journey is important for others who are faced with any kind of challenge. The will and drive to succeed cannot be underestimated for anyone determined to find a path forward. If there is a lesson to be learned from Michael's story, it is that success for any individual cannot be defined or predicted.

As a parent, there are moments in your children's lives that remain vivid in your mind. Some memories are traumatic, and April 1992 was one of those times. Michael was four and half years old when he was diagnosed with a type of low-functioning autism, which was later confirmed by two separate experts. Prognosis: Our son would not be a candidate for school, and he would need to be in a group home as an adult.

The news was devastating. Michael did not appear to understand what was happening around him. He spoke some words but not sentences. Simple questions such as "how old are you" would go unanswered. He seemed detached from his environment. Possibilities for the future were bleak.

At the time, autism was not a frequent diagnosis, and we didn't know anyone else who had personally been affected by this condition. Even Michael's pediatrician wasn't able to provide us support.

In the early 90s, autism was associated with the movie *Rain Man*, so it was a very hopeless diagnosis to be given. Articles on autism referenced "mysterious disorder" and some suggested that "punishment" may be the appropriate treatment. I was terrified for my son's future. It was clear that the perception of autism limited how others saw Michael's potential, so we decided never to use the word in describing his challenges. Instead, we would say "his left brain and right brain have difficulty connecting."

Unlike today, there was no Internet, which meant that there was very limited access to relevant information. There was no one to talk to who would say the simple words, "You are not alone." Finding help meant searching the telephone book or going to the library to research information. All we knew was that many experts had made it clear that Michael had a very challenging situation and each one confirmed his negative prognosis.

From the start, we saw more potential in our son than any testing results were demonstrating. We never gave up on Michael; and no matter how difficult the challenge, Michael never gave up either.

My own background in health care had instilled abilities that were extremely helpful particularly in those early years. The most important mission for us was to find opportunities that might help Michael develop skills he was lacking. Some things were obvious, such as speech therapy. Somewhat different than today, our big challenge was finding programs that would accept him. Due to the extent of his problems, he did not meet basic criteria for admission.

Our personalities did well with helping us persevere. Both my husband and I had very demanding careers (engineering and healthcare, respectively), and we both chose roles that were challenging. In my professional work as a nurse and healthcare administrator, I had gravitated towards roles of problem solving. My approach at work was similar to the way I tackled Michael's challenges: Set a goal and figure out how that goal can be accomplished. The main objective was to assure that our son could grow up to be a functioning adult who was able to take care of himself.

No one could have foreseen the successes Michael would find. At thirty years old, he has an undergraduate history degree, has completed his master's degree in business administration, works a full-time job, and has a full, independent life. He is a second-degree black belt in martial arts, speaks at events on autism, and sings at fundraising and other special events such as weddings. Michael's initial diagnosis was correct, but the prognosis of what he could become was significantly underestimated. Potential may not be obvious, and each person has a unique path. It is crucial that no one should be judged based on a diagnosis and its attendant preconceived limitations. That is where Michael's story may help others look beyond the negative stereotypes of autism and other disabilities.

--Joane Goodroe, Michael's mother

CHAPTER 1

A Doubtful Future

**"Courage is not the absence of fear;
it is the ability to act in the presence of fear."
—BRUCE LEE**

IN APRIL 2006, I was preparing for my high school graduation from Mill Springs Academy, a small private school in Georgia for children with learning disabilities. If a student had a more challenging disability, like I did, he or she participated in a separate program called The Communication Arts School, or CommArts for short. There were only 25 students graduating from Mill Springs, so anyone who wanted to speak at the commencement was allowed to share their thoughts. I had experienced a great number of obstacles and was thrilled to be graduating and going to college, so I wanted to give a speech. Also, I enjoyed being in the spotlight!

It was while I was preparing my speech that I first learned that I had autism. I knew I had a learning disability, but the explanation had always been that the bridge between my left and right brain didn't function well, so I would need to work harder than others. Discovering that I had autism was overwhelming, even though I really didn't understand exactly what autism was. I personally knew no one with this diagnosis and knew little about it except for what I had seen in movies. This was definitely not how I had viewed myself.

My parents' decision not to share the official diagnosis and its label with me or anyone else was complicated, but grounded on two main justifications. As they eventually explained to me, they didn't want me to be judged by the word "autism," which they believed would have limited my access to opportunities. They also didn't want me to limit myself because of the diagnosis and any excuses or barriers I may have thrown up because of it.

Years later, as I started speaking at autism events, many attendees encouraged me to write a book detailing how I overcame my many challenges. My first thought was that I didn't have any significant information to share. The reality at the time was that I didn't know the details of my diagnosis or the significance of what I had accomplished. Until I started working on this book, I had never truly understood my diagnosis and real challenges. I had read summaries of my test results but didn't really understand the implications. So, once I decided to take on this project and began a detailed review of my testing and evaluations conducted from the age of four years through high school, I was stunned by the true extent of my problems. I felt embarrassed and very sad, as if I had suffered some kind of loss. I guess I actually did in that moment, since the kid I always thought I was turned out to be another one entirely. But my parents, focusing on the positive as has been their outlook since the very beginning, quickly made me see otherwise.

I might very well not have had a story to tell had I known I was autistic. I probably wouldn't have even been equipped with the skills to share it. But thanks to my parents; a seemingly insurmountable amount of hard work and dedication; freedom from the blinders of improbability and fear; and the steadfast support of people who believed in me, I have an amazing account of unexpected positive outcomes despite my challenges. When I realized that the label "autism" had no effect on what I had accomplished up until then, any feelings of sadness went away.

When people learn that I'm leading a productive, normal life, their first comment is:

Autism is misunderstood

"You must have been misdiagnosed, or you were probably always high-functioning on the spectrum." It's these types of remarks that make sharing my testing results critical to verifying and explaining the challenges that I've faced.

As a college history major, I approached this undertaking as if documenting a historical event. I'm relying on a great deal of information provided by others in order to tell the story of my life, including reports from my intellectual and standardized testing, feedback from school records, comments from family and friends, and my own impressions. My goal here is simply to provide meaningful information to others who need hope and ideas for succeeding.

THE BIRTH OF MY STORY

From the moment I was born, I didn't sleep (this has not changed!). Six to seven hours of sleep over a twenty-four-hour period was my routine. My constant ear infections began when I was six weeks old, and to combat them I was given countless doses of antibiotics. At age three months and again at 18 months, I was hospitalized with viral pneumonia. Other than that, I was a happy baby boy. And my parents were probably really tired!

I did say individual words and some phrases but I didn't put them into proper context. My baby book describes me calling a basketball an "orange-juice ball," and I would repeat phrases from television programs. Instead of actually communicating, I sounded more like a parrot. When I was two years old, my language skills stopped progressing and my interactions with those around me also decreased. I would talk if I wanted something, but if asked a question, it was as if I wasn't there at all. Instead, I would quietly walk away. It wasn't a deliberate refusal to communicate, but, as my parents eventually learned from comments in my testing results, it was the mechanism I used when the questions were too hard for me. My behavior indicated: "I just can't do this!" I didn't cry or scream. I'd simply get up and move towards something else to distract myself.

At four years old I started preschool at Peachtree Corners Baptist Preschool, where the extent of my challenges would become more apparent in a setting with other children the same age. My cousin, Katie, who is just six weeks older than I, attended the same program. In many ways, she's more like a sister since our moms are identical twins. We also lived next door to each other back then. Both our moms worked, so we would stay together every day. My family says it was obvious that Katie was much more advanced than I was. At the time, they attributed my developmental delays to my numerous medical illnesses, and they also knew that boys didn't mature as fast as girls.

But at school my developmental delays really stood out. The teacher and principal were concerned. My mom shared their feedback with my pediatrician, who assured her that every child was different and not to compare or worry. By March, the preschool was even more alarmed and knew that the pediatrician wasn't acknowledging my challenges. They suggested that I have my speech and hearing evaluated. One particular note from the school thanked my parents for being open to their feedback and said that parents often take teachers' concerns as a negative reflection of their parenting skills. My mom and dad were just so grateful that these teachers reached out to them and started me on a path where I could get the assistance that I so desperately needed. *Early intervention*

LET THE EVALUATIONS BEGIN!

Reading the summary of the findings from that early testing was my first look at a little boy that I did not recognize as me. In a handwritten report (in cursive, which looked like something from a time capsule to me!) the tester expressed concerns about how I responded to "why" or "what" or "problem-solving" questions. Instead of answering the question, I would merely echo it back verbatim. If I did eventually respond, it was with an answer that was totally inappropriate for the question. Here's an example:

Question: What would you do if you fell in the mud? I repeated the question several times and then answered, "I just ride my bike." [1]

One part of the several-page report stated that I was unable to match identical pictures together. And when asked how old I would be the following year, my answer was, "I would be bigger and stronger." The tester ended her summary by pointing out that I made no eye contact during the entire evaluation. Her overall recommendation was that I needed a much more comprehensive evaluation to determine the extent of my problems. My first glimpse at all of this made me wonder: What was I thinking? I definitely had no idea that I had such challenges, so it was certainly a surprise to see these early details.

As a follow-up, I was sent to someone who held a doctorate of language pathology and learning disabilities to perform comprehensive testing. My mom's main concerns about me, which were detailed at the top of the report, stated that I didn't seem to comprehend what was said to me; that I struggled with communicating thoughts which were new to me; and that I was unable to answer questions when asked. I smiled when I read the next part of the report, which stated that I could remember lines from television shows and movies. Apparently, I demonstrated this ability before I was one year old!

Numerous standardized tests were administered as part of this comprehensive testing. As I began to pour over the data, I was worried I wouldn't understand the meaning of some of the terminology. But breaking it down, I found it very easy to comprehend, and it quickly became clear why my situation was characterized as "extremely challenging." The hardest part, however, was realizing that it was me that the testing was describing. I knew things were more difficult for me, but the actual documentation of the results was not how I saw myself. I always thought I was just like other children.

One of the tests was called the Wechsler Preschool and Primary Scale of Intelligence. I made a graph from the results, which makes it easier to understand. An average score would have been 90 to 109. My score was only 83, which means I was below average intelligence.

Michael's Total Score: 83
Average Standard Score: 90-109

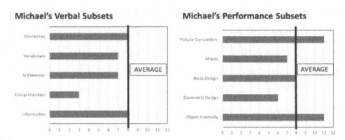

Overall, my scores were below or significantly below average in all but two categories. Significantly below average scores included those in Arithmetic, Vocabulary, and Comprehension in the Verbal Subsets, as well as Mazes and Geometric Design in the non-verbal Performance Subsets. Only my Picture Completion and Object Assembly scores fell within the average range.

My auditory processing skills were tested as well. Results showed that I had difficulty hearing subtle differences in many sounds. My strength in this area, however, was my ability to retain information. This explained my ability to repeat lines from movies that I had seen. For many years, the repeating of lines from movies was the entire extent of my speech capability. I would try to insert words from movies or television shows whenever I did try to communicate my thoughts. The testing said that I would mimic language I heard, very much like a parrot, as I said before.

The summary of the testing stated that I had "pervasive developmental delay with below-average functioning in aspects of language, visual perceptual learning, and visual-motor integration." The report also stated, "There were moments when Michael seemed to be detached from information around him." The documentation indicated that I was cooperative during testing, which my parents said was consistent with the way I acted in most situations. But it was also noted that when I was struggling with the testing, I would rub my arms and touch my tongue.[2]

As the diagnosis was e~~x~~
alarmed. However, my mom
"delay" in my diagnosis. She s
thing is delayed, it means you ~~\~~
so my mom thought I was just
that the word "delay" should ha
this for many years, so she helo
cant improvement with time.[3]

When I was diagnosed, psycl
the term "pervasive developmer
term "autism spectrum disorder'
common clinical challenges for   ~~...~~ social and
language development. However, both diagnoses acknowledged a
wide range of possible intellectual ability.

One expert explained that the diagnosis of PDD was sometimes
used when autism was present, but some of the characteristics were
mild. An example given for PDD was someone who had large social
deficits but their repetitive behaviors were not as severe. In 2013,
PDD became one of the separate subtypes of autism which was col-
lapsed into the single diagnosis of ASD. The same can be said for
Asperger's syndrome.

From everything I have reviewed about my own condition, my
testing showed below average functioning in many areas of intellectual ability with only a couple of areas where I scored in the low
normal range. A better way to describe my situation is that experts did
not believe I would be able to lead an independent life given that they
characterized my challenges as significant; and given the intellectual
testing scores, they determined that the prognosis for improvement
was not too realistic. Intellectual ability does not usually change.

OCCUPATIONAL THERAPY EVALUATION... AND MORE TESTING

Recommendations from the testing included speech therapy. My
mother, a nurse by training, also thought I would benefit from occupational therapy. The first step to any therapy was additional testing

specific challenges and customize a plan.
these tests added more information to my puzzle.
vious sessions, the therapist said I was cooperative
g and attempted all tasks. She said I appeared to under-
spoke very little. When asked questions, I would use ges-
to respond to direct questions.

During my occupational therapy evaluation, there was a platform swing that caught my interest, but I backed off as soon as I saw that it moved. The testing results pointed to a lack of balance, which also demonstrated challenges in brain function. I also tended to get up and wander off during testing. The clinical observations from the testing were summarized in a report:

Very low muscle tone.
Difficulty with equipment that required balance or movement.
Unable to maintain grip against resistance.
Hesitancy to cross the midline of the body and difficulty with trunk rotation.
Alternating movements poor with increased speed and deterioration of movement with repetition.
Developmental fine motor skills below age level.
Lack of eye-hand coordination.
Poor postural stability.[4]

The intellectual testing and subsequent occupational therapy testing identified many issues in my early development. These two reports gave me the first look into why my prognosis for a productive life had been determined to be unrealistic.

Each of the challenges identified in the testing demonstrated that my brain processing was compromised. There were so many deficits, and the negative prognosis weighed heavily on my parents. My dad found it too stressful to listen to or read the reports. He thought all that testing was doing nothing to help me, and that I was great just the way I was. My dad didn't want my life to be focused on the negative, and he has been the best father anyone could imagine.

On the other hand, my mom was looking toward the future and wanted to make sure that my opportunities weren't limited by the testing results. She realized that I needed assistance to grow and develop. She recognized that I wasn't even meeting the standards for preschool work. Although she agreed with the diagnosis that I'd been given, she didn't believe that such a devastating prognosis was a true indicator of my ability.

Ableism?

Support of Parents

CHAPTER 2

Looking for Any Open Door

**"If you think a thing is impossible, you'll make it impossible."
—BRUCE LEE**

AT THE END of preschool in May 1992, my teacher – the one who had initially identified that I had significant delays in development – summarized my performance. She stated that when she took extra time to give me directions in a one-on-one situation, I was able to follow up and attempt the work. However, I was unable to comprehend any type of instructions in a group setting. Needing so much individualized attention was a big problem. Other progress reports indicated that my letter and shape recognition as well as my knowledge of numerals was well below average. Yet, despite all that, I had completed preschool!

My parents wanted me to continue attending school just like other children, so kindergarten was, of course, the next step. Finding that next step for *me*, however, turned out to be a dilemma. While they acknowledged my challenges, my mom and dad discovered that the extent of my problems was so severe that many kindergarten programs were not even equipped to handle them, therefore they weren't able to accept me. The reality of the situation was overwhelming.

When my parents met with the school faculty, they were told that my acceptance into kindergarten would be dependent on finding a teacher who was willing to take on me and my challenges. It was a very small private program, and, as would be true for any organization no matter the size, my type of challenges created extra work and some disruption to others in the class.

KINDERSCHOOL QUEST

My mother met with the principal and one of the kindergarten teachers, Jan Bowyer. Although she was nervous, my mom was prepared. She told me later it was the first time she utilized the explanation of the lack of connection between my left and right brain to process information. This would become her strategy to explain my deficits while also trying to portray a positive picture of my long-term potential. Hoping to convince Ms. Bowyer that I could improve, she used examples of how patients who have suffered a stroke can improve brain function with therapy.

Mom deliberately kept the explanation short, thus avoiding the many deficits that could possibly paint a hopeless picture. The fact that I was not disruptive to the classroom was probably my single most positive attribute. This was true in my therapy sessions as well as my preschool classes, and it was the one redeeming and consistent facet of my behavior.

Low and behold, Ms. Bowyer accepted me into her class! She turned out to be a kind, creative, amazing teacher who went out of her way to help me and support my development. When I finished kindergarten, Ms. Bowyer was looking for full-time employment. My mom was so grateful for everything she had done for me that she wanted to give Ms. Bowyer a similar opportunity. She basically created an office manager position and hired my former teacher even though she had no experience in that type of job. I never gave it any thought when I was younger, but now I understand how important it was that Ms. Bowyer took me on as a pupil, and how deeply appreciative my parents were. This was the first example of what became a recurrent theme of how I have been able to succeed in life. Like so many others who came after her, Ms. Bowyer was willing to give me a chance.

BUILDING BLOCKS

Shortly after all of my testing had been completed, the therapists and preschool teacher met with my mom to discuss my progress. Mom was so glad to have a plan in place for both speech and occupational therapy, and she was thrilled that I had been accepted into kindergarten. She approached my future with optimism, which was concerning to the experts. They didn't think she was being realistic, given my diagnosis. A statement that was made during this meeting has forever been seared into her memory. One of the psychologists pointed to my mom's pregnant stomach and said, "You will understand how bad Michael's problems are when this one gets here." Mom, then pregnant with my brother, understood my problems, but the hardest part for her was thinking that my life would be determined by the diagnosis that she knew in her heart did not represent my "true" potential. According to my parents, this was a frightening time.

I started my first speech and occupational therapy sessions one month before my fifth birthday – a very late start according to today's standards of diagnosis and treatment. It's now known that the earlier therapy is started, the better the results. Throughout the sessions, I was reevaluated to confirm that I was making progress and new goals were set to continue my growth and development.

My kindergarten class met Monday thru Friday, but I would leave early three afternoons each week for speech and occupational therapy. My nanny, Giga, would take me to therapy and sometimes my mom would meet us for the sessions. Giga was part of my life from the day I was born. She worked with my mom as a clinical technician at a hospital and became my nanny as well as nanny to my cousins' Jenny and Katie. Giga and her mom, Olga (now almost 100 years old), are like family, and they've also played an instrumental role in my growth and development.

The goal for speech therapy was to improve both my receptive and expressive language skills. The reports stated that my weaknesses were in the areas of auditory attention and listening skills. Something as simple as pointing to pictures when given a simple direction was

Early inter-vention

a task too difficult for me to do. Strengths included my expressive language, creativity and humor. I'm not sure how they figured this out based on the report I read, but anyone who knows me would list these attributes as my current strengths today.

In speech therapy, there were initial activities that sounded very simple, but they posed significant challenges for me. For example, I was only able to identify three out of ten animals correctly when asked. Four weeks into therapy, I was able to identify fifteen out of fifteen. That sounded great until I really thought about it. For such a simple activity to be so difficult for a five- year old really said a lot about my challenges. No wonder my prognosis was so bad!

Six weeks after my fifth birthday, my brother Nathan was born. I remember being very worried about how he was going to get out of my mom's stomach and if the event would hurt her. The next day, my dad and I went to the hospital so I could meet my new brother. According to my parents, I was totally engaged in the moment and so excited to have a brother. My initial concerns about mom going through childbirth and my instant emotional response to Nathan were positive signs – reinforcement to my parents that I was very aware of my environment even though I couldn't always express my thoughts. Needless to say, my parents would hold on to moments like these, as they gave them hope for my future.

Additional testing was conducted in December 1992. The therapist wanted a greater understanding of my strengths and weaknesses so she could refine her efforts following the initial four months of therapy. She found that my receptive skills were very weak compared to my expressive skills. She noted that spatial concepts such as before, after, first, same, and different were examples of what I couldn't process. These types of words are very important in following directions, reinforcing why my issues were so predominant in preschool.

Alas, a piece of good news from the test did pop up. In expressive vocabulary, I scored in the upper portion of the normal range for my age group. Finally, an area where I was in normal range! However, both expressive and receptive vocabulary skills are essential for communication and learning. With such a deficit in receptive vo-cabulary, my expressive skills would continue to suffer.

By May 1993, nine months into therapy, the report stated that I was making steady gains in both receptive and expressive language skills. My weaknesses were in areas of auditory processing with lis-tening skills varying from day to day. In 2004, the National Institute on Deafness and Other Communication Disorders stated that "auditory processing" is used to describe the process of the brain recognizing and interpreting sound. When someone has such a disorder, some-thing is adversely affecting the processing and interpretation of the information. An example is used that helps explain how someone's hearing can be normal, but the processing of the information is not.

A person with auditory processing problems will not always hear the phrase, "Tell me how a chair and a couch are alike." Instead, they may hear, "Tell me how a cow and a hair are alike." In group settings, when there is other noise and distractions, the ability to distinguish what is being said becomes increasingly more difficult, and words can also be transposed. As I will discuss later, I've found that even now, trying to write something that is said at the same time I'm hear-ing the words is almost impossible due to my auditory processing challenge. I find that I'm unable to process what I'm hearing if I'm thinking about writing.

There's one other thing that's important to point out at this time. Every person with autism is unique – just like everyone else is unique. This means that with an autism diagnosis comes a range of different challenges and strengths. For example, many people with autism are brilliant and have no defined learning disabilities. They include great scientists, writers, mathematicians, and others. Sharing this informa-tion helps explain my situation and also demonstrates how I was able to find a path to develop. Of course, this will be different for everyone.

At five years and four months old, my average length of verbal sentences was only 3.5 words, which is about where my cousin's two-and-a-half-year-old child is today. I was shocked as I read my actual words when I tried to repeat the story of *Goldilocks and the*

Three Bears by describing pictures:

> **The Mama Bear. The baby bear sits in his chair.**
> **Cooks. Mama Bear Cook. They're playing outside.**
> **Sitting on big chair. She broked it. That bed.**
> **The baby's Goldilocks rest.**
> **He says, 'My chair broke'.**
> **Someone's tasting my porridge.**
> **Drinked it all.**
> **They broked the stairs.**
> **Someone have been sleeping in my bed.**
> **She runned.**[5]

Three months later, the therapist showed me pictures of the *Three Bears* story again, and this is what I said when questioned by the therapist:

> <u>Picture 1</u> **Michael: Where you put it? Three…the three bears and Goldilocks. The mama bear and the daddy bear and the baby bear…making the porridge…and the baby bear's is too cold. And the mama bear's was too hot. And the papa bear's was too hot, too.**
>
> **Examiner: So what did they do?**
>
> <u>Picture 2</u> **Michael: They walk outside. They do walk outside…**
>
> **Examiner: How come?**
>
> **Michael: They go around the block. They goin…mama bear, daddy bear, baby bear. They're walking.**
>
> <u>Picture 3</u> **Michael: Then came Goldilocks. Open up door…nobody home…**
>
> <u>Picture 4</u> **Michael: Eating baby bear's porridge. Try papa bear's porridge. And try mama bear's porridge. And eat baby bear's porridge.**

Picture 5 Michael: And sit on the baby bear's chair. And she break baby's bear's chair.

Evaluator: What do you think is going to happen?

Michael: Break baby bear's chair.

Picture 6 Michael: Then go up the stairs and she try daddy's bear's bed…and mama bear's…and baby bear's (Michael pointing to each bed)…and try baby bear's bed…

Evaluator: What did she do then?

Michael: Rest.

Picture 7 Michael: And baby bear says, "Somebody's been sat in my chair. And baby bear says, "Somebody's been eat my porridge. And mama bear says, "Nobody sit in my chair." …And daddy bear will fix it.

Evaluator: Why was he sad?

Michael: Because he…because daddy bear will fix it. That bear will fix the chair.

Picture 8: Michael: …(long pause)…And somebody been sleep my bed (says it three times).

Evaluator: Then what?

Michael: Goldilocks runned away.

Evaluator: Why did she run away?

Michael: Because she wants to…run away.[6]

This was a significant improvement from where I started because my sentences had moved from an average of 3.5 words to 5.8 words. Although the therapy was helping me gain communication skills, my overall development was still below average for my age, which is

obvious from seeing my words. Even thoug█
one else my age was also advancing, which m█
enough."

Once my auditory challenges were noted, this bec█
for my speech therapy. The therapist would read me a short █
graph story and then ask me to answer questions. She would als█
me to follow directions such as drawing a line up, down, right an█
left. After two months of doing these same exercises over and over
again, I was able to complete them. If I practiced something enough,
I was able to do it.

The next important goal was for me was to be able to maintain
attention in a group setting. Without this skill, it was going to be difficult for me to participate in any "traditional" school setting. The
therapist had two other children my age join our sessions. According
to the therapist, these sessions turned out to be unproductive and
distracting and simply didn't work. However, next, my cousin Katie
was invited to the sessions, where I interacted appropriately and took
turns as requested. I guess the familiarity of Katie was comforting for
me. The therapist stated in her report, "Her [Katie's] presence has
been beneficial in assisting Michael to carry over his expressive language skills in a slightly larger group."

As a follow-up to test my performance in group activities, the
therapist visited my kindergarten class. She noted that I required intense individual instructions in order to participate in group activities
such as completing a phonic workbook assignment. Once again, the
report stated I was not disruptive and sat quietly playing with a pencil or my book when I was not the one being questioned. However,
I was unable to follow directions that were given to the classroom,
had great difficulty transitioning from one activity to another, and
required directions repeated to me individually.

Moments in our lives, both good and bad, create strong memories. All therapy sessions and meetings are documented, so I've been
able to see for myself what went on behind closed doors. That's not
always necessary for my mom, especially concerning one particular

r seems like it occurred just
ɔnce again urged my mom to
limited potential. She said it
ɪce her to accept my capabili-
ɪink about the glimmers of po-
ɔm fashion, she stated her goal:
grade. Despite conceding that I
ɪpists maintained that she needed

ɔgnizing my capabilities, my mom
convinced that my auditory process-
ing was ﹍﹍﹍﹍﹍﹍﹍﹍﹍﹍ ɪy test results. She believed it was a
"different type of de﹍﹍﹍﹍﹍﹍﹍﹍﹍d that everyone was expecting me to
take a test that required hearing. If I was tested as if I were hearing
impaired, she hoped that it would reflect a higher level of intelligence
than what had been documented previously.

I was six years and one-month old when the Leiter International
Performance Scale was given. The assignments on this test didn't require hearing or auditory processing. Instead, the tasks for the test
were demonstrated rather than explained, thus taking my auditory
processing skills, or lack thereof, out of the equation. The goal was to
test my learning potential as if I were hearing impaired.

The test took ninety minutes, and it was noted that I exhibited
excellent attention throughout, which was different from my behavior
during any other testing. My actual score was 116, indicating nonverbal cognitive abilities in the high average range. This was the first time
my testing showed positive potential. The therapist reported:

**Michael was unusually persistent for his age. He worked seri-
ously and in an organized manner, and was frequently able to
correct his own errors. Though he talked a great deal of the time,
on only one occasion did his conversation relate to the task at
hand; he did not appear to be using verbal mediation to help
him. He did not miss any items below his age level and showed
particular strength in visual analysis and synthesis.[7]**

My mom was so thrilled to see the results since this was the only test so far that gave her the reinforcement to keep advocating for my future. The therapist administering the test definitely understood the significance of my results. However, she pointed out that others wouldn't consider these results as they evaluated my performance level. Since I wasn't diagnosed with impaired hearing, the testing would *not* be considered as a valid measure for me. The therapist added that my getting into a school for children with learning disabilities would still be almost impossible because of my overall significantly lower testing results. Copies of letters to therapists and teachers showed me that my mom was begging others to consider these new results.

The hole was dug deeper when, a few weeks later, I took another standardized test. The Carrow Auditory Visual Abilities Test demonstrated borderline low/average intelligence with particular weakness in sequence details with picture memory.[8] Another test showed more problems with abstract language concepts. Apparently, I could give only one concrete meaning to a word. An example given stated that, when presented with a picture of an animal called a bat, and then shown a picture of a baseball bat, it was impossible for me to grasp that both were "bats." She specified, "Michael is not able to flex quickly between changes of topic or when humor is introduced in a situation, which requires the understanding of multiple meanings of words."[9]

By November 1993, now six years old, I had completed fourteen months of occupational therapy. Of course, I'm not an expert, but I have learned that a child's physical and social growth are associated with gross and fine motor skill development. This made evaluating my progress with occupational therapy important. These were the key goals that had been targeted at the beginning of my therapy:

- Improve ability to move through space using bilateral coordination and motor planning.
- Improve attending skills as demonstrated by ability to maintain attention and shift from one activity to another and by remaining with one activity for an appropriate length of time.
- Improve balance and postural stability.

The overview of my results after being in therapy for fourteen months stated the following:

> **Michael showed considerable progress toward the goals, particularly those related to motor planning, balance and equilibrium. He has prolonged attention to activities of his choosing but not when the therapist has chosen the activity. Sometimes he appears disorganized and unable to follow directions; at other times, he is attentive with ability to perform more complex tasks. He continues to show difficulty in eye contact and lack of interactive skills. Even after over a year of weekly treatment, he usually walks past the therapist without acknowledgement or greeting and proceeds into the therapy room to find a toy to play with. In the past four months, he is in a session at times with another child. He needs reminders or modeling to talk to or interact with the other child and sometimes became so absorbed in his own play-acting that he appeared oblivious of the effect on others or the need to attend to the task. Drawings are very sparse and consist of stick figures. Right handed and switches some. Very immature radial digital grasp with pencil and crayons. Hesitancy to move across the midline of his body. He has difficulty holding flexed supine and prone extension postures, but this has shown some improvement.[10]**

In order to develop a new plan of therapy, more extensive examinations would be needed. A battery of tests was performed which identified very specific strengths and weaknesses and provided additional insight into my situation. Motor-free visual perception, somatosensory, two- and three-dimensional space perception, and praxis (the ability to plan and carry out skilled movements) were some of the areas tested.[11]

MORE GRIM FAIRY TALES

The results of the extensive testing were summarized as: General Integrative Dysfunction and Dyspraxia on Verbal Command, with the bleak statement, "The only area where Michael did not show dys-function was in visual perception."[12]

What is dyspraxia? It's defined by the National Institute of Neurological Disorders and Stroke as "impairment in the ability to plan and carry out sensory and motor tasks."[13] It's explained that indi-viduals with the disorder appear "out of sync" with their environment. Symptoms vary and may include poor balance and coordination, clumsiness, vision problems, perception difficulties, emotional and behavioral problems, difficulty with reading, writing, and speaking, poor social skills, poor posture, and poor short-term memory.

It was interesting to read that I had much lower scores for the left side of my body, especially in the areas of kinesthesia (awareness of body movement), standing and walking balance and motor accuracy. My other behaviors were described as: "Shows aloofness or unaware-ness of others; flat affect; little eye contact; preoccupation with cer-tain topics; difficulty in knowing how to relate to other children; talks in 'scripts;' preoccupation with TV or movie characters; large prob-lems sleeping and fear reactions to some sounds. Loving and sweet child without acting out behavior problems."[14]

Scores and explanations from the test were and are helpful, but it was pointed out on a separate page from the traditional report that there was one rather interesting finding. The testing consisted of two parts: a very simple test and a complex follow-up. The therapist said that I actually scored better on the more complex part. She specu-lated that the initial introduction on the first test helped me on the second, even though I didn't satisfactorily accomplish the first task. This was another point that did not escape my mom's attention.

The next words in the report gave my parents more hope concern-ing what I could accomplish in life. The therapist wrote, "Michael's underlying deficit may not be as severe as the total indicates. Instead, Michael may need time to process the demands of the task and then organize himself to meet them."[15] Hanging onto these words rather than the devastating report as a whole was how my parents kept mov-ing forward and advocating for my next step. The most disappointing

21

aspect for them was that others would consider only test scores to determine my school readiness and not the possibility that my deficits may not be as severe. Being denied access to the traditional opportunities for children because of my very low scores was the reality.

At this point, the concern remained that there may not be any school at all that would accept me for first grade. The only thing left to do was have a developmental physician evaluate me. The Emory Marcus Center had just opened in the Atlanta area and I saw their physician. There, other types of testing were utilized that confirmed an overwhelming list of challenges. These are some brief highlights from the summary:

Michael's verbalizations, or answers, tended to be prolonged in response time. Michael took time, even when he answered appropriately. Sometimes his answers were on target to the topic on hand. Often his answers were tangential, that is, related but coming off a tangent. Often, they were associative and sometimes totally unrelated. For example, in the middle of the phonology testing, Michael made a comment: "I hate Ninja Turtle shaving cream." At one point he interrupted the testing to ask about my ring. At several points in the testing, Michael became echolalic, that is, repeating things that were said, often repeating the instructions as if to clarify them to himself and to reassure himself. At times he became echopraxic of movements that I used for demonstration. Michael tended to maintain an open mouth posture throughout the testing.[16]

Testing was categorized into three areas, with the following results: (1) visual motor integrative skills below average; (2) language processing tests showed significant deficits in receptive or understanding skills and particular deficits in communicating, particularly complex language use; and (3) significant social interaction difficulties. The original diagnosis of pervasive developmental disorder resulted from three areas of dysfunction: impairment in reciprocal social interactions; impairment in verbal and non-verbal communication and in imaginative activity; and a markedly restricted repertoire of activities and interest.

Based on the evaluation, the physician suggested medication, an antidepressant used to treat children with nerve conduction disorders and insomnia. I took three doses of the medicine, and my mom decided to discontinue it. She said I was sweating heavily and looked like I had the flu. She was afraid it would create new problems instead of making anything else better. It was the only time that any medication was used to treat my autism and learning disabilities.

One of the recommendations from the Marcus Center was that I take another hearing test, which I did. The results confirmed that my ability to hear sounds was normal. Each new expert who evaluated me sent me for yet another hearing test, even though the first one was normal. This repeat testing despite normal hearing results demonstrates that something about my situation was perplexing to the experts. Barage of testing.

Eighteen months after speech therapy was initiated, it was time for the Wechsler Preschool and Primary Scale of Intelligence test…again. By now, I had likely won "Most Tested Child" Award! Compared to my first testing, the same pattern of strengths and weaknesses emerged, except my score on Object Assembly fell from average to borderline. That meant that, despite my new skills from all that therapy, based on my age and attendant expectations, I had not developed at all. However, there was one area of good news! My overall vocabulary rose from low average to average.

More specifically, the test showed that I demonstrated significant strengths in the ability to identify the missing element in a picture, which required visual attention to detail and visual imagery. Difficulties included my inability to correctly label parts; mazes and block design; and any fine motor coordination such as drawing.

I was able to define some words but demonstrated confusion with others. These are some examples of my attempt to explain:

A hat: that's where you wear on your head;

A leaf: that's when it comes down on a tree;
A castle: where you build is made out of sand;
A castle: is that has a kingdom;
A holiday: a day is where a Christmas.

Note also the lack of correct sentence structure. I demonstrated confusion about question forms and often gave an associated but incorrect response, as seen here:

What shines in the sky at night? "Sleep."
What goes on a letter before you mail it? "In a mailbox."

Word retrieval was also a problem as noted in these examples:

A stem was a grow;
A step on a ladder was a climb;
The leg of a table and clothes pins were handles;
A ruler was a weight measure. [17]

Without this documentation, it would be impossible for me to understand what I was like and to explain my challenges to others.

As was the case with many other documents reviewed to better understand my past, I found certain words highlighted in this devastating report from twenty-four years ago. It contained one sentence that my parents wanted to remember and share with anyone who would listen. The therapist wrote: "Because of Michael's severe language problems, the obtained scores should be considered a minimal estimate of his intellectual potential."[18]

FINDING FIRST GRADE

Based on all the information gained from the developmental physician and therapists, my mother applied to the three recommended schools for first grade. She also sent applications to every private program in the Atlanta market that had classes for children with learning disabilities. Her hope was that I would be accepted *somewhere* in light of the fact that a developmental physician had suggested at least several schools. One of his recommendations had been a school mainly geared toward children with severe behavior problems. He had pointed out that this would be the last school to consider since my challenges were not behavior related.

Reading copies of the applications and cover letters gave me insight into my mom's efforts to portray my situation in the best way possible. She outlined the words from my testing results using quotes from therapists stating that my potential may be greater than what the testing showed. She was being a great salesperson, and my positive future potential was what she was selling!

All of the schools except one sent rejection letters back as soon as they received my application. Two letters made it clear that my diagnosis and testing made me ineligible. One letter stated, "…Michael's language problems and behavioral issues are more significant than our first-grade population. We serve a mild to moderate learning-disabled child and Michael's diagnosis of pervasive developmental disorder indicates multiple problems." In other words, my disability was *NOT* mild or moderate.

The second rejection letter addressed their concern of me even going to school when they wrote, "(We suggest) that Michael continue with independent therapy sessions that are suited to his particular needs." Between the immediate rejections and these two letters, it was obvious that my testing scores were going limit my ability to move forward. In essence, getting into a first-grade program focused on children with a learning disability proved to be a much harder task than most can imagine. My problem was more than a learning disability!

After a few weeks, my mom contacted the final school that had not rejected me to see where they were in the review process. It was the one that the developmental physician did not highly recommend for me. The school said that they would be evaluating the possible fit and be back in touch.

Two months after the application was received, they asked us to come for an interview.

My dad, mom and nanny went with me. The school was not a traditional looking school. Instead, it was an older single-family home converted into a school with a couple of small buildings around it. The entire student population for first through twelfth grades consisted of about fifty pupils.

My dad described the moment we walked in the front door as the "worst feeling he could have." Two adults were trying to keep a child on the floor from harming himself. They were wrapping him in a straightjacket and the student was screaming. My dad and my nanny wanted to leave. Since my mom knew that the school treated children with severe behavior problems, she wasn't as surprised but agreed that this wasn't the best first impression. Remember, this was a school that handled children with behavior problems in addition to intellectual ones.

The founder of the school, who everyone called Tweetie, wanted to talk to me first. She led me into her office, which was dark and completely covered in books from floor to ceiling. I have no memory of what she actually said to me. Instead, I remember looking at all the stuff in her office. Next, Tweetie asked to see my parents. She had very few words for them other than to state that I didn't possess any ability to communicate. My mother said later she just knew that these words would be followed by a rejection. Instead, Tweetie followed her one sentence with, "We will take him as a student." That was the end of the conversation.

As we left the building, I was looking around and not really hearing the conversation between my parents and nanny, which makes sense as I didn't follow a lot of what was said around me at that age. My dad said that there was no way I was going to that school, and my nanny strongly agreed with him. Mom said that there were no other options, and we needed to try it. Mom won the argument, *as usual*. With that, I would have two months until school started.

Knowing I was scheduled to start first grade at Mill Springs Academy, the therapists began to wrap up the final two months of preparation for my next step. My final testing showed some improvement in my expressive description language and also improvement of my comprehension and sequencing of eight-line stories. I answered sixteen out of sixteen questions correctly. This is how I told the story of the eight-line paragraph that the therapist had read to me:

This is about two boys. They were in fishing. They smelled smoke and where it was coming from. They runned...find out where. They runned to the cave. They found fire and then they found... they went back to the lake—get some buckets of water. They put out the fire. They want to get some cold water to help the fire get away. Help out out the hot.[19]

I was able to sequence the various elements of the story correctly, but it's obvious that I had difficulty linking one thought to another. I continued to struggle with prepositions when they were used in directions, such as *between, behind, in front of, next to,* and so on. It was noted that if the activities were repeated from one day to the next, I retained the information. However, I wasn't able to retain the information when tested several weeks later. The therapist believed that my difficulties with prepositional concept contributed to my problems in following oral directions. The following explained my progress with reading:

Attempts were made to introduce Michael to 'sight reading' technique to support his ability to learn to read. However, seeing letters on a card does not seem to be effective for Michael. Instead, he seems to respond to books that use ten words in the book which include context clues, picture clues and humor. He is a type of reader that utilizes repetition and visual and auditory memory for additional cues for learning these sight words. There are three combinations of techniques used to help him learn to read: sight word approaches, context word approaches, and phonic analysis. Each is helping Michael develop a separate skill set.[20]

In addition, it was clear that words with multiple meanings, ambiguous sentences, and figurative language were all too abstract for me. This is what I call the "concrete" brain of someone with autism. When asked to tell a story about a picture, I could only repeat what I'd heard someone else say. I had no ability to come up with my own description. There was no abstract thinking at all.

By the end of June 1994, two months before I started first grade, I had demonstrated the ability to be in a group setting, stay on topic, answer specific questions, and control my impulsive behavior by waiting until it was my turn. The final occupational therapy report highlighted my progress, stating that my greatest improvement had been in my ability to move "through space with appropriate motor planning." Examples included planning a sequence of activities involving skilled motor activity with movement, and doing a series of tasks while moving on the swing. However, I always wanted to repeat the same activities and wouldn't think of any variations without assistance.

An important improvement noted was my ability to integrate auditory-motor functions such as following three to four steps. This was referred to as my "auditory sequences for motor activity." My muscle tone and general postural stability had also improved. For fine motor skills, the Peabody Developmental Motor Scales showed that I was at 4.5 years—eighteen months lower than I should have been. I had difficulty buttoning medium-sized buttons, folding paper and managing paper clips.

The final area noted was my level of attention, which was characterized as "variable performance." Sometimes I had good contact; other times, I tended to wander around the room. I worked best in a structured environment and seemed to be motivated when another child was in the room participating in the same activities.[21]

Delving into my documented past at age twenty-nine, all of the information presented about this soon-to-be-first-grader was new to me. As mentioned earlier, I never understood the depth of my challenges, and it took several months for me to go through everything. It made me feel overwhelmed and very sad, so every once in a while, I had to stop and later find the energy to go back and learn more about this part of my life. Ever the cheerleader, Mom continued to point out how far I've come.

Despite being overloaded with a laundry list of negatives peppered with only a few positives, my testing results became the foundation upon which I was to build my future. Such a shaky foundation supported only limited next-step opportunities for me, but you have to start somewhere. I have been able to succeed in spite of it all! Seeing where I started and where I am today should give hope to anyone having difficulties in certain areas of their lives. It's important to just take that next step...

CHAPTER 3

Consistently Earns Fabulous Friday

"The possession of anything begins in the mind."
—BRUCE LEE

WHEN I STARTED first grade, there were five other students in my class with two teachers. Again, I attended a school known to serve students who had both intellectual and behavioral disabilities. Because my only behavior problem was the inability to stay focused, I actually had one positive thing in my favor when school started.

Although I was in a special learning environment, to me it was just like any other school. Now I understand that the very high teacher-to-student ratio created an environment that was tailored to the requirements of children with additional needs. Also, the school made some things less stressful on students such as having all teachers and faculty addressed by their first names.

The initial negative impression my parents experienced with Mill Springs disappeared as soon as school started. The first thing they noticed was a caring group of teachers that embraced each child. In addition to recognizing and working on areas that needed improvement, the teachers saw the positives in each of their students as well. And the parents were so grateful that they had found a school for their child. This created a common bond, and my parents were thrilled that I had ended up in a place where I was embraced and nurtured.

First grade started out with another test called the Swassing-Barbe Modality Index, utilized to determine which method of teaching would be best for me. (This would be my last standardized test until the end of 6th grade!) On the Visual Perceptual scores, I was ranked in the lower 30 percent level for my age group, and on the Auditory Perceptual scores, only in the 10 percent level. As expected, my visual skills were better than my auditory ones. I was turning seven years old when first grade started. Looking at the individual segments in the visual area, my parents found a few bright spots that gave them hope:

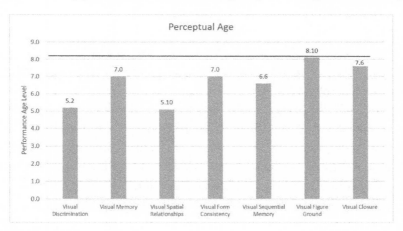

The Auditory portion of the test demonstrated very concerning areas such as Auditory Number Memory and Auditory Word Memory where I was not even performing at a four-year-old level. As my mom and I reviewed these testing results for this book, she mentioned how she was gaining a greater understanding of what some of these tests were demonstrating. She said that, at the time, it was very hard to understand the details of so much information. In sum, these tests gave a lot of information, but it was difficult to put the entire picture together.[22]

Significance of positive Reinforcement, from first person perspective

SCHOOL OF HOPE

Mill Springs offered a unique model to help students understand expectations, provide feedback, and reward positive effort. It was originally designed for behavioral problems, but it worked well for all types of goals that students were working to achieve. A weekly feedback sheet tracked overall performance, which included academic effort, behavior, participation and other relevant information. These feedback sheets were instrumental in helping me trace my progress for this book. A student could earn points each week that would determine if he or she qualified for "reward" activities at the end of that week. Being able to participate in "Fabulous Friday" was a fun, motivating goal. Earning daily points also gave a student immediate access to an extra break during that school day.

In addition, a "level system" rewarded students based on the completion of academic work, overall behavior, and social interactions. Everyone started as a Level C, where many remained their entire time at Mill Springs, as moving to Level B wasn't easy. As a basic consideration, one would need to meet goals each week. Level B students were rewarded with lunch off campus each Friday, so it was a big deal. Students could also be demoted to a Level D, which had other consequences, such as being suspended.

Weekly reports were reviewed with each student and also sent home so that parents could keep track of their child's constant progress. This also helped parents enforce goals from week to week. The feedback sheets were completed by both the student and teachers each week. This enabled kids to learn to take responsibility for their actions instead of it just being a one-way communication with only the teacher completing the information.

On Fridays, all the teachers and students would gather together to provide feedback to each student. The school did a phenomenal job teaching its pupils how to support each other and provide positive responses. There was no such thing as a "bully" at Mill Springs. Instead, each child's uniqueness was part of learning to celebrate diversity.

My first weekly feedback sheet stated that my personal goal for that week was: "I will learn the point sheet." Each sheet included comments from teachers, like this one from that very first week:

Michael had a super first week! Michael is working on recognizing shapes and working with manipulatives (mathematical objects). Michael has learned two new songs, "New Friends" and "Days of the Week." Michael has also been working on writing his name. We are looking forward to a wonderful year.

The following chart depicts the actual weekly goals from my first school year, and the number of weeks I had to focus on each one. For example, for one week, my goal was to stay focused. Seven weeks out of the year, my goal was to stay on subject. These goals were very challenging for me. However, it helped direct my attention to one key item each week with structured feedback on what worked and where I needed to try harder.

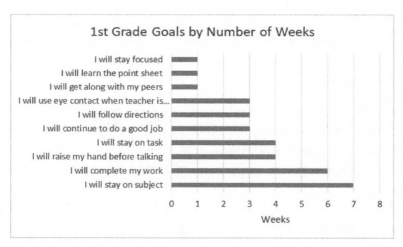

At the first parent-teacher conference, the principal of the lower school (grades one through three) and my two first-grade teachers went over my progress report. It was so positive that my dad said at the end of the conference, "Sign us up for the next twelve years at Mill Springs Academy!" I was in good hands. I had a place to grow and develop.

The first quarterly progress report highlighted my overall performance for the fall. My consistent and frequent strengths and also areas that needed improvement are summarized here:

- **Consistent strengths: sits appropriately, has materials ready, does not insult, abuse teachers or students (remember this was a school for behavior problems at the time), ignores insults from others, very courteous behavior**
- **Frequent strengths: positive attitude, follows directions, controls frustration, asks for help when needed**
- **Needs some improvement: stays on task, raises hand to speak, ignores distractions, asks pertinent questions, responds appropriately to questions, initiates positive contributions to group discussion, works independently, verbalizes feelings**

There were also written comments that supplemented the above areas. Some of the key comments include:

Positive: Learned to keep place when reading. Enjoys learning about the world. Enjoys music and very attentive during entire class time.

Areas Needing Improvement: Does not make inferences from reading, unable to put thoughts into writing and has difficulty dictating to teacher. Math work inaccurate. Still struggling with right and left concept. Unable to copy items and does not have appropriate spacing.

Even with all these continued challenges, the week-to-week reports were positive overall, which kept me feeling good about myself, and my parents feeling like I was on the best possible track. Because I was getting positive feedback, I was completely unaware of the depth of my challenges. I definitely didn't see myself as others did.

My positive efforts and behavior were rewarded with me being promoted to a Level B the first week in January. I was doing the work assigned. The school didn't penalize me for my learning challenges and being behind other students my age. Also, I exhibited positive behavior. It was such a highlight for both me and my parents. I was excelling at something! Part of my responsibility as a Level B was to serve as a role model for other students. This was a big deal. I had succeeded at moving to Level B because I had worked hard to meet my goals, had completed my assignments, and had followed the rules. I had been able to accomplish something that many others in my school had not. This was the greatest feeling for me, and no one was more excited than my parents.

By the end of winter quarter, March 1995, my strengths and weaknesses were similar to the previous quarter with the following reported:

> **Michael is using his finger to keep track when reading. He likes to read aloud. Reading 35 DOLCH sight words. Must use his fingers for counting. Difficulty completing work until he has mastered the concept. Continues having difficulty asking questions. Does not grasp cause and effect relationships.**

My inability to communicate was obvious to my teachers but not to me. If I didn't understand something, I didn't know how to tell someone. I also couldn't "read between the lines."

Mill Springs was one of the first schools to implement laptop computers for each student. Using a computer keyboard was a new skill that would be important to me because it would replace the immense challenge I experienced in writing out a simple letter from the alphabet. However, the report I found surprised me. I had the impression that this was a strength of mine because it was so much easier than using a pencil. It appears that my initial attempts to coordinate and replicate movements with my eyes, fingers, and mind would prove to be difficult, as this report shows:

> **Introduced keyboarding with all categories needing improvement including: problems with eye-hand coordination, spacing, fingers to keys correctly, reproduces text appropriately, very slow speed.**

At the end of March, I had requested feedback on what it would take for me to move from a Level B to a Level A. As a result, both my accomplishments and areas in which I needed improvement were outlined for me:

Accomplishments: Consistently earns break, consistently earns Fabulous Friday, good effort on academic task, positive attitude most of the time; appropriate level B lunch manners

Needs Improvement: Work on staying focused on subject during group activities; in Art, work on staying on task and not wandering around the room; continue working on being a good Level B role model; continue working on appropriate interactions with peers especially during less structured time.

Looking back on these areas that needed improving provides great insight into my coping behaviors at the time.

My last weekly feedback sheet for first grade on May 26, 1995, demonstrated that I was finding a different way to cope with my environment, and it was *not* good news. "Michael has been less in touch with reality this week (black Spiderman and a traffic policeman)." Although no other documentation on this was seen at this point, my socialization skills were not developing at the same rate as other children, so I retreated into a world that worked for me. When I was encouraged to participate in conversation, the only thing I knew to talk about was what I call "my stories," which were basically random compilations of lines from movies and shows that I used to concoct into scenarios in my mind. I can honestly say that I thought this was appropriate when I was asked to participate in activities.

By the end of first grade, I had made improvements in some areas but my challenge areas had become more illuminated:

Mastered 96 out of 108 Dolche sight words [which provides a solid base for reading at an early base]: difficulty in drawing conclusions and making inferences. Unable to conquer simple

sentence structure. Math is difficult and he needs encouragement to continue to work on assignment. For the year, social studies and science life has been a very strong area for Michael. Does not stay on task when working independently but will start working when reminded by teacher. **KEYBOARDING: Has learned the basics of keyboarding and is now reproducing characters as instructed.**

Keyboarding removed the challenge of writing for me. Just making myself write one simple letter in the alphabet was a lot of work. And when I tried to write, I wasn't able to listen. It was exhausting for me. Not having to use my energy to write allowed me to focus on the assignment and not the task of trying to make my hand work to write each letter.

I earned Fabulous Friday each week of the entire school year. This demonstrated that I was a student who did what was asked of me each day. I also maintained my Level B, which further showed that my behavior was not a problem. I have never wanted to do the wrong thing, and I found a letter from my first-grade teacher that substantiated this, even at that young age:

> *Becky and I wrote this letter because Michael was <u>very</u> upset by the fact that Dad would be angry with him for doing bad. This incident was not really anything to be concerned about except for Michael's distress; we would not have even mentioned it to you. We think Michael is overreacting to this incident and want to reassure him that he did the right thing by resolving the problem appropriately.*

Dear Dad,

Today at break I called Neil "Mom." It made Neil very angry. He decided to push me away after I had hugged him. Neil misunderstood my hug—he thought I meant to hurt him. We both went to Becky's office to talk it out. Becky was so busy with someone else

so we started talking about it ourselves. We apologized to each other and decided to be friends. Then we also decided what to do the next time. I would tell Neil that I wanted to hug him. Becky said that students are in her office often for problem solving also for doing good work. Becky, Neil and Michael feel this problem is completely solved. I handled it well and Neil accepted my apology and we are friends and I accepted Neil's apology, too.

We wanted to let you that Michael handled this problem like a Level B, and also that there is probably no need for follow up at home. We felt there is no need for punishment at home because Michael handled it at school.

I do want to clarify that my dad has been endlessly supportive. He wouldn't have been mad at this incident, but I didn't want to disappoint him. I see this same trait in myself even today.

Overall, the first-grade year was positive for all of us. In particular, I had succeeded in areas such as behavior and effort. My teachers were pleased that I had progressed with my academic goals, even though I wasn't performing at a first-grade level. There were no standardized tests at the end of the year, so we had a positive outlook about my potential. I also attended summer recreational camp at Mill Springs with Katie, where I received the award for Most Improved Positive Participation, another encouraging milestone. As far as I was concerned, so far so good!

CHAPTER 4

Lost in Autistic Translation

"Always be yourself, express yourself, have faith in yourself; do not go out and look for a successful personality and duplicate it."
—BRUCE LEE

STARTING SECOND GRADE, my very first feedback sheet provided a revealing glimpse of what had been a challenging week. My goal had been to stay on subject, but I had had great difficulty staying focused and needed to be redirected. Afterwards my teacher had instructed to me to write a sentence on the report explaining my less than stellar performance. She went on to say, however, that I had a positive attitude about trying harder. The sheet also shows that I had been sick that Monday and Tuesday. I had so many ear infections as a child, and each one seemed to further compromise my auditory processing ability.

The next week was better, as I met my goals and earned my breaks. By the fourth week, a new goal was set to help me address my lack of communication skills: I will talk about things related to the class. Apparently, I had found my voice, but I didn't have the ability to connect my words to the situation. Instead, I would bring up my own topics, such as movies and superheroes, which had no relation to anything happening at school. It was impossible for me to understand the difference between simply talking and actually communicating.

I was staying on track until the week of October 20th, when I started showing increased difficulties in areas such as following directions, staying on subject, talking about non-related things, and also needing to walk constantly. The walking has always been my way to "unwind" my body; apparently, this behavior was in high gear. As a consequence of this bad week, I was dropped back to a Level C. My behavior was not an example of a Level B anymore. After that blow, my behavior and work improved. The only way for me to climb back to a Level B was to consistently meet my new goal, which was to stay focused on my work. Being dropped to a Level C had bothered me a lot and I was on a mission to succeed, so my December comments were glowing.

The first two weeks in January were also terrific, with my teacher writing, "Michael is doing so well! He has been so positive about following directions and completing his work." By the end of that month, however, my goal was changed to "I will have verbal self-control." According to the reports, my comments at school remained unrelated to the environment I was in. I was never aware of what staying on subject actually meant. When I was asked to participate, I had no understanding of what I should say or that my comments were inappropriate. I thought they were asking me to talk more. It was so confusing to me. Autism simply does not allow one to understand the nuances of some things, as I will discuss in more detail later.

I was sick again the first week in February 1996. Although I had met the goal of staying on topic since November, after my illness, the comments stated that I was very distracted. As we reviewed this information, my mother, who was going over the files with me, explained that any type of short illness always seemed to make it harder for me to focus afterwards. It was like climbing a mountain and sliding back down again.

By the end of February, I was back on track according to the positive remarks on the feedback sheets, which continued into the next month. This was a sign that I was showing consistency in my positive behaviors. Finally, in mid-March, I was promoted back to a Level B and my goal became, once again, to continue being a role model for my peers.

AUDITORY CALAMITIES

As I reviewed the information from April of my second-grade year, a very memorable occurrence from my childhood surfaced. I had told the teachers that I would be getting a dog on the last Saturday of the month. My dad had written it down on a calendar back in November when he was teaching me about the months of the year. The reason this was so memorable was that on that last Saturday in April, I said, out of nowhere, "This is the day I get my dog." My parents replied, "Michael, we are not getting a dog." I was quiet for about thirty minutes as I tried to understand why I wasn't getting my dog. My next comment was, "When I have a child, I will not break my promise to him." My mom, sensing that there had been a big misunderstanding, asked me why I thought I was getting a dog that particular day. I went to the cabinet and pulled out the calendar, where the word "DOG" had been written on the last Saturday in April. My dad quickly clarified that he was just using it as an example to show me how to use a calendar. I had remembered the date and never mentioned it, except at school the week before. Mom looked at Dad and emphatically told him we *were* getting a dog that day.

The story of the dog demonstrated several things. I understood the concept of what my dad was trying to teach me, but I didn't hear or understand everything he said clearly. Obviously, my auditory processing skills compromised what I heard. I also didn't talk about how I was looking forward to the dog or other things that were regular topics of conversation, demonstrating how any type of dialogue was not part of my skill set. The reason I said it at school was that I was specifically asked on Friday what I was looking forward to doing over the weekend. Of course, getting the dog was on my mind! The thought of having a dog had been a source of excitement since November, when my dad wrote it on the calendar. However, as was my nature, I kept that excitement to myself. In the end, I did get that dog – a Golden Retriever puppy I named Zeo after a character from the *Power Rangers* television series with which I was obsessed.

I successfully completed second-grade, with the requirement for special reading tutoring during the summer. One of the teachers worked with me to assure that I wasn't falling even further behind than I already was. Reading was worse than difficult. I never could hear the sounds of the letters so it never made sense to me when I was asked what sound a letter made. Visually, it was hard for me to distinguish the letters so reading a word was challenging. I was disappointed that I had to work even harder on my reading over the summer. Reading felt like a punishment, and I knew my cousins weren't going to have extra classes during the summer like I did.

THIRD GRADE: TREASURES AND TRAGEDY

While reviewing materials from third grade, I found an essay I had written that was an answer to the question: What is your treasure? My essay was comprised of two sentences, and I know I had help on the spelling because it was correct. My answer: I have come so far on working on my own. This is my treasure.

I'm sure my answer was unique compared to others. I guess I remembered that working on my own was a goal of mine, so that's what I associated with the word "treasure" instead of writing about something I enjoyed, like going on vacation or playing. Fast forward twenty some-odd years and my third-grade essay answer really surprised me. As mentioned, this entire process of reviewing testing and performance comments, seeing my actual work, and hearing my parents' memories of my grade school experience has been very strange. I just had no clue that I had so many challenges.

Looking back at my records, I also see that my perception of how I was doing overall in certain subjects was quite skewed. For example, I believed I had excelled in keyboarding. As I mentioned earlier, Mill Springs was one of the first schools to adopt a "laptop" environment in order to assist many of their students with different learning disabilities. Typing a letter from the alphabet was so much easier for me than writing it. However, to my surprise, my third-grade progress reports demonstrated a dire need for improvement in both speed and accuracy compared to what my peers could do. I had always told people that I had no trouble in this area. I guess when I compared my challenge to writing a letter of the alphabet versus how much easier it was for me to type it, it seemed to me that I had mastered the skill. My perception was different than reality.

Throughout third grade, I maintained a Level B with no difficulty at all. It was noted that I always earned breaks and Fabulous Friday privileges, and that I was also seen as a good role model in how I treated new students. However, I wasn't eligible to become a Level A at the time as I still needed to improve my ability to stay on task ("Sometimes his mind seems to wander."), and participate more in class discussions.

Although I was making progress academically, I wasn't keeping up with the development of others. Donna, who was one of my teachers, suggested increasing my tutoring during the school year. I remember being so disappointed that I had to go to school all day and then be tutored. As usual, I didn't voice my opinion. I just kept it to myself.[23]

Third grade was the end of the lower school at Mill Springs. I would now transition to the middle school, but not without chaos. The wood-frame home where the school had been located burned to the ground one night. Atlanta was a fast-growing area, with an equally accelerated demand for a school focused on learning disabled children. Fortunately, within days, Mill Springs had managed to acquire land in a less developed area and moved temporary school rooms to the sight. Mill Springs was growing and developing, just like I was.

LITERARY ASPIRATIONS

As far as I knew, the transition to middle school wasn't difficult for me. Of course, anyone reading my reports could see that I had areas of substantial concern, but they weren't obvious to me because I was being evaluated based on where I started and how I was doing. First of all, I maintained a Level B my entire fourth-grade year. This demonstrated that my behavior and overall responsibility level were very good. These are the summaries of my performance written by the teachers:

> **Reading: Michael has worked on making inferences and drawing conclusions which he struggles with as he perceives things quite literally. He needs to work on learning to ask questions. I love his enjoyment of literature. He is working on his comprehension and vocabulary. He has a difficult time staying on task and working independently.**

> **Language: Michael struggles with written expression. He needs to work on sequencing his ideas, writing in complete sentences, and spelling. He does have a good command of words.**

> **Math: Michael has worked on addition and subtraction and consistently is 85%-90% accurate. He is having difficulty with fractions.**

> **Science and Social Studies: Michael requires a great deal of attention in order to retain the material. Has trouble staying on task.**

> **Drama: Michael has enjoyed drama. He has an active imagination and participates consistently.**

> **Michael has some great leadership skills. At times, he has a problem making a statement that sounds "on-subject."**

By the end of the fourth grade, a general update stated:

> **Needs to work on inference skills and learning to ask questions. Michael struggles to get his thoughts on paper in a well-developed paragraph. Michael has shown a surprising knowledge in science. Michael has done well in history and has a nice sense of humor. Michael is working well with WORD and is improving with practice. Great participant in music. Doing well in group activities.**

This summary of my strengths and weaknesses could have been written today. I've always had trouble getting my thoughts on paper. The funny thing is, I love to make up stories more than anyone can imagine. I see a scene in my head but struggle to get it onto paper. I obtained a college degree in history, and I do love music. I think I have a great sense of humor, but I'm not sure what made the teachers say this in their summary. It shows that, despite what I've been able to accomplish since fourth grade, I really haven't changed!

Documentation from the beginning of fifth grade relayed that I was doing better with reading but having difficulties pulling out clues for characterization and motivation. "His biggest problem is inference and author's purpose," reported one teacher. In other words, my thinking was concrete. *This is your brain on autism*—often literal and cannot draw conclusions from something that has not been experienced first-hand.

By the end of the year, I did make progress. The documentation stated that "Michael enjoys all reading genres. He is an enthusiastic participant. His comprehension skills—predicting events, drawing conclusions, understanding story elements have all improved." Yet, expression in written form remained difficult. It was a target area for improvement and efforts were made to help me learn to use more descriptive adjectives, nouns and adverbs.

Some examples I found of my attempts to expand my use of adjectives made me laugh. I would learn words that were adjectives and then just use them randomly in sentences. "When I woke up, I felt gloomy that today was a weekday…It was not going to be a comical day," I wrote. In a letter to Santa, I penned "I have been a fascinating boy this year. During school I have completed all of my homework. I am especially superb in math. Every week I see Donna for tutoring. I am learning to be infinitely better when writing…" In reality, my use of adjectives is still very concrete, but I've gotten infinitely better at it!

In math, I had difficulty grasping the rounding of numbers, a concept that is not concrete. However, it was also stated that "Michael was a wonderful math student, always very positive and giving his very best." Despite my issues with rounding, I was deemed ready to move on to the next level in mathematics.

To me, math was a subject in which I was doing great. When the teachers or my parents told me I was doing well, I thought it meant that I was a great student – top of the class. All these years, I knew things were harder for me, but I always thought I was performing at grade level. It was probably helpful to my self-esteem and overall dis-position that I didn't understand just how far behind my performance was compared to that of other children my age. I now wonder if I would have stopped trying.

I was contributing in science class and had positive comments on my thought process related to the subjects we studied. I also enjoyed social studies. My grasp of subject-specific content broadened, and as a result, my academics began to improve steadily.

While the reports included a heartening list of my consistent strengths,[24] my greatest at the time fell under the category of Values, which didn't pertain to any one class but to my general behavior throughout the school day. Here are my teacher's comments on that:

Michael is an ideal member of our group. He enjoys our discussion and demonstrates great maturity in making appropriate decisions. He is so much fun to have in class.

By spring semester, the Values section of my report also included this: "Michael is contributing insightful comments to his peers during group feedback time. We all learn from him." The fact that I was able to engage in appropriate feedback to individuals was a huge step forward.

There were important comments in physical education (PE) as well. The same teacher had taught me PE since the first grade. Her comments demonstrated a meaningful, positive change in my skill level:

Michael had a super semester—best yet! He seemed interested in all activities, participated at a high level and his skills with

each new activity/game/sport presented were terrific. I'm very proud of Michael and all of his accomplishments this year.

At Mill Springs, positive behavior was rewarded. At the end of fifth grade, I received recognition for both singing in the talent show and "most improved" in math. Sixth grade, which was the final year of middle school at Mill Springs, also proved to be an affirming experience, as evidenced by progress reports from my teachers.[25] At the end of sixth grade, I received the P.E. Shining Star Award and the Enthusiastic Story Teller Award.

Overall, middle school fostered an optimistic view about my accomplishments, and my parents and I were feeling good about the achievements I was making. To me, my struggles were no more significant than those of other children. I was even on the honor roll for the entire sixth-grade year and had maintained a Level B with no difficulty. Of course, honor roll meant I had performed well at my specific level…not my grade level.

On the surface, it seemed as if I had very few challenges. However, in reviewing my science journal, it showed that I was still unable to write a complete sentence without assistance. My school reports were not comparing my performance to that of other students. Instead, I was being graded on my goals of moving forward. When I look at my actual work, I now understand that I had many, many deficits.

For my parents, a huge highlight of sixth grade was my participation in the school talent show. I sang "I Can Go the Distance," by Hercules. I definitely did *not* understand the significance of that song at the time.

CHAPTER 5

Fast Track Backwards

**"A goal is not always meant to be reached;
it often serves simply as something to aim at."
—BRUCE LEE**

IT HAD BEEN six years since I had taken any type of standardized test. Maybe that's why I thought I was doing so well in school! At the end of sixth grade, students were given the California Achievement Test, which, for me, once again dispelled any thoughts that I was at least an average student. In Reading, Language, Math and Total Battery, I scored below the national average. My performance wasn't even *close* to average in these key areas.

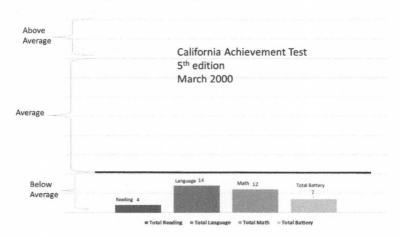

Further details were provided on my performance in the different subsets. Under Reading, my Vocabulary score was only in the 2nd percentile, and my Comprehension was in the 6th percentile. If I'd guessed on the correct answers, I would have done better. Under Math, I scored in the 13th percentile in both Mechanics and Concepts/Applications. In other areas, I managed a 19th percentile in Science and 27th in Social Studies.

Ever the cheerleader, my mom pointed out that I was close to low average in Science and was in the low average range for Social Studies. Wow! These scores were really bad. But we had to deal with the reality that they would dictate my steps as I transitioned into junior high school. I was already in the slow race, but now, I had fallen way behind again.

NOT FLOURISHING AS SOCIAL BUTTERFLY

In September 2000, I turned thirteen years old, which made me an official teenager. I entered the pre-upper program at Mill Springs, which was the beginning of seventh grade. Even though I had very low scores on my standardized testing, my parents and I were not too stressed because I had progressed in middle school, indicating that I was moving forward on my academics and had also been role model for behavior.

Another problem quietly surfaced, however. It wasn't highlighted as much in the reports, but my challenges in social skills were only increasing. Even at Mill Springs, it was obvious to others that I had bigger issues than just learning disabilities. These issues boiled down to a lack of communication and a lack of awareness of what was happening around me, which added up to zero, as in *no* socialization skills. Definitely the hallmark of autism!

There were also changes occurring at Mill Springs. It had been growing into a much larger school for students with mild to moderate learning disabilities. I had a *major* learning disability. Plus, the number of students attending the school was increasing, as well as the types of activities the school offered its students. The pre-upper

Comorbidities .

49

program was faster paced, and I can remember feeling like I had entered into an entirely new and challenging realm. My seventh-grade experience would crush my belief that I didn't have any more challenges than other students. In writing this book, I have learned that my parents were also jolted back to the reality that my path was in fact strewn with obstacles. Things began to fall apart right from the beginning...

Mill Springs always included students in every meeting with parents. Their belief was that the child needed to take an active part in every discussion so that he or she could take responsibility for finding ways to meet goals. At our initial meeting with the principal and teachers of pre-upper, the faculty outlined their high level of expectations. They even acknowledged the fact that many students have a hard time transitioning into seventh grade. Also discussed, the trials of becoming a teen, the life stage when new challenges arise for *all* people. So, it would make sense that *I* would endure new problems during this transition also. My parents tell me now that they left that meeting with grave concerns. They didn't hear the reassurances that had been given in the past. Instead, they heard why this was going to be almost impossible for me to handle. Their premonition was correct.

Only six weeks into school, there was a much-anticipated ten-day trip to Europe for pre-upper students. I had traveled to Japan with my parents, so they were hopeful that I would do fine on this school trip. As it turns out, I didn't do well at all. Of course, I had no idea that I had problems on the trip. From my standpoint, I had participated in every activity, enjoyed the sites, but did miss home. I didn't, however, relish all of the food, and I shared my thoughts. However, I wasn't at all aware of the way I was perceived, which is very typical for someone with autism. I definitely didn't – couldn't – read the social cues. This is one of the comments written by a teacher after the trip, addressed to my parents:

Michael had a difficult trip. He seemed to enjoy the sites but was continually making comments about being homesick. We do not

discourage this but he became very obsessive when asked not to discuss it as much. He was not very aware of his surroundings and at times, needed to be more courteous to the public. He got strong feedback about being inappropriate and he seemed to do much better afterwards. Overall, Michael needs to work on his social skills.

Here, I must share feedback from my mom. In traveling abroad and being away from my parents for so long, not all had been a disaster. In her mind, I had demonstrated a set of life skills that had not been obvious to her before that trip. Each student was allowed to bring a certain amount of money for fun spending. Everyone except me had spent all their money before the trip was even half over. I, on the other hand, had completed the trip with money to spare, even after buying snacks at the airport for classmates who had spent all theirs. I had also purchased presents for my family and relatives, which my mother described as thoughtfully chosen and selected. On my return, she was thrilled that I had shown these types of life skills. Managing money is something that many people aren't able to do effectively. In addition, I may not have shown awareness of my surroundings in general, but when I was buying presents, I demonstrated a different kind of knowledge and awareness of those around me.

The week after the trip, a meeting was scheduled with just my parents, which was very unusual. Initially my parents believed I was being penalized for something that happened on the trip despite so many years of good behavior on my part, but that never came up. As it turns out, the school wanted to move me from the pre-upper program immediately into a program called Communication Arts (CommArts) that Mill Springs had established several years earlier. This came as such a surprise to my parents. CommArts represented a huge setback to them, one that was forcing me off of a track where I had been succeeding. They had no knowledge of the CommArts program at the time, other than the fact that students with more severe problems were part of that program. They were crestfallen that I might be one in need of this kind of assistance.

My mom told me about the plan to move me out of pre-upper immediately. I was devastated because I felt like I had done something very wrong. I've never cried so hard in my life. I kept saying I was sorry and Mom just kept assuring me that I had done nothing wrong and that CommArts was going to help me develop some other skills. My parents never told me until now how upsetting this move had been to them. It was hard for all of us. I'd been happy where I was, and my parents had also been excited that I had been given the opportunity to proceed on a positive track. They were worried that CommArts would be yet another barrier.

An objective review of the information now makes us realize that the move was based on both my low standardized test scores and my lack of social skills. I was not an appropriate candidate for pre-upper. Being so far behind academically and socially, I needed a more individualized approach. In the long run, CommArts turned out to be a blessing.

The CommArts program included twenty-five students from seventh to twelfth grade. The emphasis of the program was on social skills and communication. When people would use the words "social skills and communication," I had no idea what they meant. I guess if I *had* understood what they were talking about, I wouldn't have had difficulties in those areas to begin with. By definition, when a person has autism, there is a lack of ability to be aware of their social challenges; telling someone they need to work on those challenges has absolutely no meaning if that someone is autistic.

Although the teachers and Kay, the principal, were extremely supportive of the students, I was now back on a Level C (where everyone had to start) and couldn't understand what I had done wrong. It felt like I was being punished for no reason at all. I just didn't comprehend what was expected of me, and why the rules had changed from what I had been doing for the past six years. With my personality of wanting to do the right thing, stress and sadness seeped in. I guess being a teen didn't help either!

At least some aspects of my new environment were similar to

what I had already experienced at Mill Springs. The academic classes were taught by teachers in CommArts and other parts of the school, and students attended each class based on performance levels, not specified grades. My initial subjects included math, language arts, life science, and social studies. But I was with new teachers and the adjustment would be rocky. In addition to academic classes, there was also a focus each day on communication skills and social interactions. This was the biggest change.

Reviewing the seventh-grade feedback sheets reminded me of another challenge that I faced transitioning to CommArts. I was receiving positive comments from all but one teacher, in the life science class, who wrote, "Michael does not bring his materials to class," and "Michael says he does not have the book that I distributed at the beginning of the semester." After my experience in Europe, I was afraid to say too much, but the teacher kept insisting that I stop making excuses. When my mom saw the feedback sheet and I told her I had never been given a book, she immediately helped me straighten out the problem. This may seem very trivial to most, but for me it was difficult understanding what was acceptable to say. Even today, I struggle to understand what is and is not appropriate. I try to apply what I've learned, but it doesn't always make sense to me.

In CommArts, students had both a social and an academic goal each week. These goals were either next-step opportunities or derived from feedback identifying areas in which a student needed additional focus. My first goals were to get back on Level B and to make new friends. Both would prove to be very challenging.

It wasn't long before I knew all the CommArts students' names, yet it was much more difficult for me to make friends as I moved into adolescence. I guess I was unable to pick up on the more advanced social cues that were critical to developing relationships. It was noted that I wasn't recognizing others' personal space. I was unaware of what others were doing when I approached them (I interrupted a lot of conversations!), and I also moved physically too close to them. This kept me at a Level C, which was very challenging for me.

It's hard to explain how difficult it was for me to understand what was meant by "personal space." My dad finally helped explain it in terms that meant something to me. He told me to pretend that I was not to penetrate a person's "force field." He had me hold out my arm to help me think about the field that I should not enter. This made sense to me! Space now had a definition that I could apply to a situation. My behavior in this area improved immediately.

In January, one of my classes was theater. I've always loved living in the fantasy world of movies and stories, and was now in a class where this was actually the goal – very exciting to me! The feedback was nothing but good news. The social rules didn't apply and communication was scripted. What a great combination for someone like me.

By the end of seventh grade, I still hadn't made my way back to Level B, which was very disappointing. I'd done great academically (based on the goals that had been set for me), but social challenges continued to hold me back. This bothered me a lot and I was more determined than ever to figure out how to make it to a Level B and then ultimately to a Level A.

In eighth grade, I was on track with my goals in CommArts. I had also been moved into a couple of classes with other pre-upper students, which did a lot for my self-esteem. I felt like I had finally overcome some of the concerns that had sent me to CommArts in the first place. Then, one month into eighth grade, I was promoted to a level B. This made me feel so much better about my performance. I had achieved an important goal of mine and was now serving as a role model again. I would have no difficulty maintaining this level for the rest of the year.

Robert Moore, who has been headmaster of Mill Springs Academy for twenty years, recalls an instance that epitomized my dedication to getting ahead, as well as my mother's fierce advocacy: My science teacher, who was also an advanced chemistry teacher, insisted that I could not have done the work that I presented from home. The next day, Mom and I had an appointment with the teacher. She urged me to open up my laptop and bring up the PowerPoint. "Explain to your teacher how you did this," Mom insisted. I complied and went through the assignment. The teacher remarked, "Good work!" Then she walked out; that was that.

"That teacher became another believer that Michael Goodroe was capable of doing good academic work," Moore said. "This helped some of our teachers understand what true capabilities look like. They don't always look like what you would expect."

STEP ON THE INTELLIGENCE SCALE

In preparation for high school, it was time for more professional testing in order to develop a fresh plan for my particular needs. It would also establish any special accommodations for the school and teachers to consider. Such accommodations are critical in ensuring that students have an opportunity to succeed. It had been eight years since I had taken an IQ test, and my parents were hopeful that this new series would show significant improvements in some areas. As for me, I was – thankfully – completely unaware of the outcome of all of it until I began work on this book.

The comprehensive testing occurred over four sessions when I was fourteen years old. As part of the testing, I met with a psychologist who provided input on her interactions with me.[26] Also, my teachers and parents had answered specific questions about how I was performing at school and at home. Feedback from my science class, for instance, stated that I had been doing well, and highlighted that I was in a regular classroom setting, not CommArts. Several teachers described me as enthusiastic and hard working. It was pointed out that I responded well to individualized instructions. My grades were A's and B's, and I was respectful and well-behaved in school. It was highlighted that I was not tolerant of classmates who were disruptive and did not follow the rules. Another comment stated that I demonstrated caring traits toward my classmates and I was well-accepted, despite my weak social skills.

From my parents' standpoint, they stated that while I had never tested well, I had accomplished quite a lot. They also wrote,

"Although it may take him longer than most students, he has always met the goals that were set for him. He is motivated to learn and do well in school. He has not presented behavioral concerns in school or at home. He always does his homework, although he needs assistance from us. Michael has difficulty understanding what he reads on his own, but he is able to comprehend it better when it is read to him. We will read the text with him and then help him with notes. On an assignment that requires writing, Michael does better if he can dictate his thoughts. He has difficulty formulating and organizing his thoughts and getting them on paper on his own. He spends at least two hours a night on homework even though the school thinks homework should take no more than thirty minutes." [27]

One of the tests administered was the Wechsler Intelligence Scale. Results demonstrated that Intellectual Abilities were at the low average range overall. My test score was 87, which was in the 19th percentile, with a Verbal score of 90 and a Performance score of 86. There was a 95 percent probability that my true IQ score was within the range of 82-93.

The subset scores can range between 1 and 19 with a scaled score of 10 being average. These subset evaluations always presented a different picture than the total score. In the Verbal Scale subset, I scored below average in all categories but Information, where I scored within the average range.[28] The second group of subsets, Performance Scale, represented an enormous variation in scores, with Picture Arrangement as a strength, and Coding at the very low end of the scale.[29]

Index scores, which were derived from the Verbal and Performance Scale subtests, were used in place of IQ scores. Skills analyzed included Verbal Comprehension and Perceptual Organization, which both fell in the low average range at 32nd and 39th consecutively. In comparison to other testing, this was an improvement. Freedom from Distractibility, at the 10th percentile, was below average, and my Processing Speed was extremely low, a 70, which put me in the 2nd percentile.[30] These last two areas showed significant deficits in performance. The formal report further explained the results:

Michael's verbal comprehension skills were within the average range, overall. An area of comparative strength was noted in his fund of general information, which was within the high average range. Michael's abstract reasoning skills were within the average range. His vocabulary was within the low average range. Michael's common-sense reasoning skills were within the borderline range. Michael's perceptual organization skills were within the average range, also. An area of comparative strength was noted in his nonverbal social reasoning and sequencing skills which were within the high average range. His puzzle assembly skills were within the average range and his alertness to visual details was within the low average range. Michael's visual analysis and synthesis skills used to reproduce block designs were within the borderline range.

Michael scored in the low average range on those subtests which were most sensitive to concentration and impulse control. This included short-term auditory memory and mental computation. Michael's short-term auditory memory was within the low average range and his mental computation skills were within the borderline range.

Michael's processing speed was within the below average range and it was an area of comparative weakness for him. This was measured by his speed and accuracy in visual learning. Weaknesses in this area may affect his ability to complete assignments in a timely manner.

The results of the intellectual evaluation indicated that Michael's mental abilities were within the low average range, overall. Generally, his verbal and visual/spatial abilities were within the average range. He had more difficulty on tests that were sensitive to attention and impulse control and processing speed. Michael's processing speed was within the below average and an area of significant weakness for him. A slower processing speed may affect his performance on timed, standardized tests and his ability to complete tasks in a timely manner.

The psychologist applied my testing results to what was important to help me succeed in high school. She said that I required time to complete assignments. One accommodation recommended that I receive extended time for testing, particularly group-administered standardized tests such as college entrance exams. She also pointed out as my strengths the amount of information I understood and my nonverbal social reasoning skills. Both of these were within the high average range.

Yet another test administered, the Wisconsin Card Sorting Test (WCST), measures nonverbal reasoning skills, problem-solving strategies, cognitive flexibility and ability to use feedback in problem solving. This test examined my executive functioning ability or, in essence, my ability to function in life. I scored within the average range, completing all 6 categories in 118 trials with 92 correct responses. The detailed results of the WCST indicated that I exhibited good nonverbal problem-solving skills as well as the ability to learn from experience. This is definitely what my parents always saw as strengths in me. My deficits in this testing included difficulty with maintaining the response set and weakness in attention and impulse control, which the tester thought may have affected my performance on the test.

My language comprehension skills were also assessed. The Peabody Picture Vocabulary Test-Third Edition (PPVT-III) provided a measure of my comprehension of a single word presented in isolation. My score of 94 was in the 34th percentile with an age equivalent of 12 years and 4 months. (Remember, I was 14 at the time.) This was considered within average range. The Listening Comprehension subtest of the Wechsler Individual Achievement Test measured listening skills more typical of those required in a classroom. This one demonstrated a lower score of 87, the 19th percentile, with age equivalence of 10 years and 3 months, which was the low average range.

My expressive language skills were measured utilizing the Picture Vocabulary subtest of the Woodcock-Johnson Test of Cognitive Ability-Revised (WJ-R COG). I scored in the average range with a 103, 57th percentile and age equivalent 14 years 7 months, which was within the average range. The examiner did point out that I was not able to have a conversation with her. She described it as "Talked at examiner rather than with her."

My auditory perceptual skills, which had always been a huge issue for me, were assessed using the Incomplete Words subtest of the WJ-R COG. I was asked to identify a word from an incomplete presentation. My score was only in the 3rd percentile with a 71 and an age equivalent of 6 years and 4 months. Apparently, at age 14 this remained an area of great weakness for me.

The summary of my language skills demonstrated test results within the low average to average range, which was a slight improvement over previous test results. Two areas of significant weakness were conversational speech and auditory perception. The auditory perception was believed to affect my ability to accurately hear and understand what is being said. This made the classroom particularly difficult for me where there were competing noises and distractions.

The next part of the testing assessed many things. In visual processing, I performed poorly overall.[31] Next up, my visual motor skills, which resulted in a score of 83, which was in the 13th percentile with an age equivalent of 9 years 6 months, within the low average range.[32] Verbal and visual memory, including both immediate and delayed, were also assessed, utilizing the Children's Memory Scale (CMS). My general memory score was 81, 10th percentile, which was low average. On that entire test, there was only one area where I scored within the average range: my ability to learn new material quickly. I had a score of 109, which fell within the 73rd percentile.[33] This is what my parents saw in me and why they kept pushing me forward.

More testing showed that my reading decoding skills were below average at a beginning sixth grade level, and both my reading comprehension and math computation skills were only a fourth- to fifth-grade level. Math reasoning clocked in at the fourth-grade level, and my spelling skills, which were identified as an area of significant underachievement, placed in the second- to third-grade level. The report's summary was as follows:

When asked to write a passage, Michael's written expression fell within borderline range and at a third-grade level. He had particular difficulty with sentence structure, use of punctuation, spelling and handwriting. Michael's writing skills were significantly below the level expected given his intellectual potential. These results are indicative of a specific learning disability in written expression. Difficulty writing may affect his performance in any class that requires the writing of essays or papers.

Michael's borderline to low average achievement in reading and math was commensurate with his low average to average intellectual potential but somewhat low. Given the extensive academic assistance provided by his school, one might have hoped for higher scores. Michael's low frustration tolerance may have negatively affected his scores. He seemed to have a certain comfort zone with academic work and appeared unwilling to push himself much beyond this point. This was he would make comments such as, 'My head hurts when I see something too hard.' This also may affect his classroom performance. Michael may be comfortable with working at a somewhat lower level of expectation.

After reviewing this part of the report, I had to stop working on this book for a while. It was just not how I had viewed myself, and it made me very sad. I knew I put more time into my homework and classwork than other students, but I had no idea that I was performing at such a low level. I'm just so thankful I kept trying.

Testing continued with the examination of my attention level, impulse control and planning. The evaluator stated that I tended to respond impulsively and was easily frustrated, but that I also appeared attentive. Noting the somewhat inconsistent pattern of my scores, she suspected the presence of some distractibility and impulsivity. She stated that "this was consistent with previous evaluations which also cited concerns regarding Michael's ability to control his attention and impulses. However, neither Michael's parents nor his teachers reported concerns regarding his attention span."

To complete the testing, my social and emotional state was also reviewed using interviews, checklists, and projective techniques including drawings and sentence completion.[34] The report stated:

Significant impairments were noted in Michael's social skills. He did not appear able to engage in the reciprocity required for social conversations. His thinking is rather concrete and this also may interfere with his ability to interact socially. Michael appeared to have the desire for social interactions but somewhat on a limited and superficial basis. He made some comments indicating concerns regarding friendships and happiness, but he would quickly back away from these comments and report that everything was fine. For example, he stated 'I'm a smart guy. Why don't the smart guys have friends? The smarter you get; the more happiness goes down.' However, he quickly followed that statement with: 'I'm happy with what I have now…friends and family.' When asked for three wishes, Michael stated that he could not think of any wishes because he was 'happy with what I have now.' However, when the request was restated and made more concrete by asking him what he wanted for his future, Michael replied that he wanted to become an actor, have a family and be a martial arts instructor. There was no evidence of anxiety or depression. Michael appears to be a caring and concerned adolescent with difficulty with social relatedness. These impressions were consistent with the previous diagnosis of Pervasive Developmental Disorder.

The final part of the report was very important in determining my next steps in high school (and, as it thankfully turned out, college!). Based on my testing, I qualified for accommodations to help me succeed. The recommendations included extended time for both tests and the completion of assignments; teachers' notes/outline to follow during class; a word-processing program for assignments and note taking; the option for oral exams; and taped versions of textbooks (in addition to printed) when available.

The psychologist also said that it was important for me to be encouraged to set higher expectations for my academic achievement. She was concerned about my level of frustration, and she thought I was comfortable not pushing myself to the next level. In order to accomplish these higher expectations, she suggested that my teachers raise *their* expectations. She also suggested increased participation in regular (not CommArts) academic classes such as history or math, in addition to regular science class. Finally, the expectation for my future education was addressed:

> **Based on the results of this evaluation, Michael and his parents may wish to consider a two-year college certificate program or a vocational training program rather than a four-year college after high school. Michael may use high school as a time to refine some of his interests for a career in the future. He already has an interest in being a karate instructor and this may be a reasonable goal for him.**

It was a soft way of saying, "He does not have the ability to attend college." Although it was not recorded as part of the testing process, my mom remembers having a discussion with the psychologist concerning high school. The psychologist had doubts that I would be able to keep up with a full load of high school classes. She suggested moving me to a part-time status.

CHAPTER 6

Fighting Spirit

"As you think, so shall you become."
—BRUCE LEE

BEING UNAWARE OF my very negative testing results while I was growing up was a good thing. It's hard for me to imagine what it would have done to my self-esteem had I understood the extent of my problems. My parents still refer to the continuously negative testing results as a "kick in the stomach." The only way they continued moving forward was to not think about the implications from the testing. In their minds, as long as I was going to school, I was making progress. They didn't permit the actual test results to interfere with my day-to-day life.

My mom also found continued inspiration from stories of people who had succeeded in spite of their challenges. She would share the information with me and my teachers. One of her favorite examples was an article titled "Overcoming Dyslexia" in *Fortune* magazine (May 2002). It began with, "Consider the following four dead-end kids."

One of the people highlighted in the article was Paul Orfalea, the founder of Kinko's. The article states, "[Orfalea] failed second grade and spent part of third in a class of mentally retarded children. He could not learn to read, despite the best efforts of parents who took him to testers, tutors, special reading groups, and eye doctors." Orfalea refers to the fact that his mom was constantly telling everyone that he was more capable than people thought he was. (It sounded like my mom!) When working on group projects in college, he would offer to do photocopying, binding and other activities that didn't involve the writing of reports. As Orfalea took on the coordination of material for his group, he realized there was a market opportunity that wasn't being met, so he created Kinko's business model. By providing an array of copying and binding services and other office needs, Orfalea became a tremendously successful businessman.

In addition to Orfalea's story, the "Overcoming Dyslexia" article contained many more examples of people who became highly successful despite their bleak beginnings. When my mom first showed me the article, I assumed that dyslexia was much worse than my challenges. It reinforced for me that others were struggling also. In 2002, when the article was written, negative opinions abounded concerning the potential and capabilities of someone with dyslexia. This article, as well as other efforts over the years to highlight people who have overcome dyslexia, have changed the negative assumptions that once surrounded this diagnosis. Hopefully, people with autism will also be seen in a more positive light as stories of success emerge.

For those highlighted in the article, and for me, what leads to success isn't always obvious. But my parents and I know for a fact that one thing has made a significant positive contribution to my life – Taido Karate. I was about five years old when I first saw Bruce Lee in a movie. He flew in the air, moved with swift precision, and was everything I wanted to be. Not only did I think I could be like Bruce Lee; I was already a little Lee in training, as I had been enrolled in a martial arts program while transitioning from occupational therapy into first grade.

I wasn't able to participate in a group sport activity because of my limitations in motor coordination and communication, so my parents went searching for some type of physical activity that would work for me. They found it just down the street from my house – a martial arts program called Taido. Its enduring, positive impact on my life is a certainty, but, like everything else in said life, the benefits would not be immediately obvious.

TAKE THE PATH LESS WALKED

In 1994, there were no studies that supported the concept of martial arts as a therapy for someone with autism. But what was obvious to my parents was that martial arts provided many of the same types of benefits that countered my weaknesses. The physical, mental and motor development activities in martial arts were similar to exercises I had received in occupational therapy. This particular martial arts program worked with all different ages, so my cousins, Katie and Jenny, would be able to join the classes also. The big question was: Would I be accepted into the martial arts school with my challenges?

When my cousins and I attended the initial class together, the first thing I noticed was that every student wore a *gi*, a martial arts uniform, and they were all working hard on their movements. The chance to actually be one of those students was like going to a movie and thinking I could be in it. I knew that the owner and main instructor, who everyone referred to as Sensei, was from Japan, and I wondered if he knew Bruce Lee. In the black and white poster-size pictures of Sensei that hung on the walls, he certainly *looked* like something out of the movies. He was flying through the air in one picture and another showed him breaking a large stack of concrete blocks. This was everything I wanted to do and be!

Mom, Auntie Jeane and my nanny were watching the three of us work out. Of course, Jenny and Katie were right on target with their ability to follow direction and carry out moves. Apparently, I was unable to even follow the simplest move where you take both arms and make a downward gesture. One of the assistant karate instructors continuously worked with me throughout the class, to no avail. My mom said she was so upset seeing how I struggled with such a simple command. It seemed hopeless, and was heartbreaking for them to watch. They just knew there was no way I would be invited to become part of the class. Afterwards, Auntie Jeane asked to speak to the head Sensei to plead my case. She explained my challenges and asked him to please consider accepting me. He said he was willing to give me a chance, but I had to show that I possessed a willingness to try, or, as Sensei always said, "do my best." In other words, I would be allowed to stay if I showed that I wanted to learn and improve.

To say Taido has played a significant role in my life is an understatement. Even the history of this program is important to my story. My martial arts school, which was the first school of Taido in the United States, was started in 1975 by Sensei Mitsunobu Uchida who has a seventh-degree black belt. Taido was created by Dr. Seiken Shukumine, Uchida Sensei's instructor when he was growing up in Japan. Shukumine personally chose Uchida Sensei to head up the program in the U.S. This single decision by Dr. Shukumine has had the most profound impact on my life because someone else may not have been willing to give me an opportunity.

Over the years, Uchida Sensei has developed the school into a family-run business, with two of his sons joining him as instructors. The school has grown to more than 400 active students of all ages and backgrounds. Most of Taido Karate's students stay and continue their progression. In essence, they have created a place where everyone feels like they are part of something special. I, for one, certainly do!

Understanding the impact that Taido has had on various facets of my life requires a basic understanding of this particular brand of martial arts. Taido training is based on sets of complex movements that are put together to form a *hokei*. Students start with the simplest hokei and continue to build towards very integrated, complex movements. There are five techniques in the Taido hokei. *Untai*, which is the body axis moving forward and then retreating, is the most basic. (There are also more than just those two advance/retreat movements because the body can be at many different levels.) Next, s*entai* is the turning movement, which is combined with both upward and downward movements. Then there's *hentai*, complex changing of the body axis involving leaning and deliberate toppling over with a very specific style. There's also the twisting of the body axis, known as *nentai*, which is similar to a whirlpool-type movement both in the air as well as on the ground. Finally, there's *tentai*, which involves cartwheel-type movements and twisting. In this stage of training some students, able to perform complete turns in the air, resemble advanced gymnasts. For me, simply performing a cartwheel was and is an enormous accomplishment.

Taido is different from other martial art styles in that the techniques require the body to adapt to a changing axis while focusing on balance of the entire body. To be successful, it takes a great deal of training, focus and concentration. When you consider my challenges, martial arts represented exactly what I could *not* do. I had poor balance, did not move across the midline of my body, and had great difficulty processing complex directions, not to mention that they were given in Japanese! But I had been given a chance, and I was determined to try my best.

HOKEI, HERE WE GO!

Although I had been accepted as a student of Taido, watching my struggles was difficult for my family. When I was standing next to others, my deficits seemed magnified, thus highlighting the obstacles I faced even more than simply reading the reports from my formal testing. But as a happy "Little Lee" in training I was oblivious to the impressions of others. Sensei Uchida assigned a black belt student to work one-on-one with me each class. Despite that, one month into class, I had not yet learned the basic one-step technique that other students master in ten minutes. But I stuck with it. Sensei would say in his authoritative, motivating tone: "Michael, never give up!" No words have had greater meaning in my life, and to this day, I continue to hear his voice whenever I face a challenge.

In the beginning, even the simple warm-up exercises before class were impossible for me. Take the "bridge," an exercise that requires coordination of the abdominal muscles to stabilize the body in order to arch the back upwards from a position laying on the floor. Descriptions state that anyone can learn to do it, but it took me six or seven years to execute, reinforcing the great difficulty I had engaging my muscles. Yet, I persevered. Two or three times a week, I was at martial arts. I didn't realize it at the time, but it was therapy for me. Martial arts training, in general, is known for increasing self-control, focus and listening skills, which had all been identified as important target areas of growth for me in my weekly goal sheets from school.

With almost no muscle tone, an inability to move through space, and lack of balance, coordination and motor skills, there was nothing about martial arts that was in my favor other than the inspiration to be like my hero Bruce Lee. I also wanted to be like my new heroes, Sensei and the black belt students in my class. I was determined to keep at it even when I seemed to take longer than other students to learn something. I was so focused on trying to follow instructions and on getting my body to respond that I was completely unaware that no one else required additional support or took as long to learn things. Just like in school, I was blind to the fact that I was significantly behind everyone else's performance. Yet, in spite of my slow progress at Taido, I maintained my vision of becoming a martial artist who could star in movies. Every time I put on my gi, I was hopeful that the talent locked inside would come out.

For all students, Uchida Sensei structures Taido to reward "best effort," which encourages each individual to keep trying to succeed. His philosophy is to measure students based on their time and effort in meeting new goals and their own personal growth. This kept me going as long as I didn't compare myself to others. I saw Katie and Jenny soar through the basic techniques. Sensei did everything to assist me in my growth, but I was also trying as hard as possible. One of the things that assisted my progression through the initial exercises was being next to Katie and Jenny. I attempted to copy their movements instead of trying to process the verbal command. It was difficult enough performing such complex and challenging movements, so taking the verbal processing out of the mix helped.

Every student starts with a "white" belt. When Sensei determines that a student has accomplished certain tasks and is proficient in certain movements, a test is given. If successful, a student advances from a simple white belt to a white belt with red stripes. With each belt color, there are three levels of stripes to achieve. With eight belt colors and three steps within each belt, there are twenty-four different steps that must be achieved before reaching a black belt. Before each test, Sensei, with great conviction, would state the words "Do your best."

Just like other students, I had to complete all training. Once I learned untai, the first level, the next one, sentai, which requires turning movements, added new challenges and complexity for me to conquer. In addition to the individual hokei, students were expected to perform group hokei in unison. This also provided a huge challenge for me because, in the early years, I was so much slower than other students. But after many years of training, I was able to participate in a group hokei just like everyone else.

Taido had tournaments twice a year. While Katie and I both competed, we had distinctly opposite performances at these tournaments. She was very talented in Taido and would always win a medal or trophy. On most occasions, she placed first. She advanced to a brown belt very quickly. It was hard not to envy her ability. However, a life lesson for me would eventually emerge. Katie's many talents prompted her to participate in lots of different activities, and she dropped out of Taido to pursue another sport. Although she had great ability, her accomplishments with Taido ended in seventh grade with a brown belt. I, on the other hand, continued!

When I was ten years old, U.S. Taido competed in Japan. Our family joined a group of other Taido families for this unique experience. I didn't win any medals but still felt like I was part of something special. On the trip, I noticed that other children my age were sitting together in the back of the bus. I wished that I could sit with them, but I thought I had to sit with my parents so my brother wouldn't be by himself. I didn't understand, at the time, that I had not developed the social skills to join others my age.

A very memorable event occurred on the trip. Acting on an

impulse, I hugged the grand master of Taido, Dr. Shukumine, while he was onstage. Two things wrong with this move: It was an event in a formal setting, and he was not someone who expected a hug! Apparently, he was in the midst of a ceremonial bow and I ran over to hug him. My parents were stunned by my quick decision to get to Dr. Shukumine, and they immediately started to apologize. His daughter spoke English and said, "It's okay, that was very nice." Upon his death years later, several people commented that I was the only person who had ever given him a hug. The reality is that, in spite of my lack of intuitive social skills, I was attempting to show him my appreciation and respect. I wanted to thank him.

Ten years into Taido when I was fifteen, it was announced that I was a candidate for my black belt as I had mastered all five techniques. Just being a candidate was so exciting for both me and my family. Not only was I entering my freshman year in high school; I was working on my black belt, which made me feel very good about myself. Before my sixteenth birthday, I earned that black belt in Taido. The level of pride and accomplishment I felt is hard to explain. It was one of the greatest accomplishments of my life. My parents said that I looked just like every other student who got their black belt. It had been a goal of mine, and I had made it!

During those first ten years, there were so many people that started Taido. Many, like Katie, were extremely talented but a great number of them didn't continue their training. Not only did I have a black belt, but I was one of the few who had made it to that milestone. This is such an important lesson in my life. Success is not just about ability. It's also impacted by continued effort and hard work. It didn't matter how much longer it took me to earn a black belt. In the long run, I stayed with it. Mine is the modern-day version of *Aesop's Fables' The Tortoise and the Hare*. I finished the race that many with much greater ability did not.

When I started martial arts training, there was no research demonstrating its positive effects for people with autism. It wasn't until 2010 that the University of Wisconsin released study information on

Reference article?

the benefits of martial arts for children with autism. In general, the study showed that it improved motor skills, balance, coordination, communication skills, and self-esteem. It's believed that the intense structured exercises lead to increased skills in concentration, and that the activities in martial arts also helped children with autism engage socially with others.

Results from another study were published March 2016 in the *Journal of Autism and Developmental Disorders*, titled "The Effect of Karate Techniques Training on Communication Deficit of Children with Autism Spectrum Disorders." The group of research participants who engaged in karate techniques training for just fourteen weeks showed significant improvements in their communication deficits compared to others who did not participate.

The study confirms what happened to me. The repetitive movements with a disciplined approach was a form of therapy. In the movie, *Karate Kid*, when Mr. Miyagi instructed Daniel to paint the house and "wax on, wax off" the car, the boy was becoming more disciplined and building more muscle in the process. This is exactly what happened to me at Taido. By allowing me to go at my own pace, Sensei assured that I had mastered one skill before trying something new.

In addition to developing my discipline and my muscles, there are other things about Taido that I consider invaluable. As mentioned before, there are limited group activities for someone with autism. With Taido, I was always part of the group, both during class and on Taido outings. One thing I looked forward to each year was the summer beach retreat for both students and their families, when we participated in intense sun-rise workouts near the waves followed by belt advancement awards. It was a time of hard work and celebrating accomplishments with everyone else.

There are very few activities like Taido where any family member, regardless of age or talent, can participate together since each person is judged on their own ability and each person advances at their own pace. My brother joined when he was five years old and then my dad started classes a few years later. Now all three of us have earned our black belts, and twice we have travelled together to Japan to compete. There aren't many activities in life that would allow three very different people to be together in such a way.

Just like me, Taido grew over the years. One of Sensei's sons, Mitsuaki, eventually became the head instructor. When he was only seventeen years old, he would encourage me, but he also made me work very hard. At times, when I couldn't master certain moves, he would give me individual lessons in our basement. Mitsuaki is now married with two children of his own. He's been a friend and a great mentor to me. Now, his dad doesn't break the concrete blocks, he does. I admire him, and I know that so many others do also. Mitsuaki has never made me feel like I was different or less than anyone else. Like his dad, he's helping people in many ways.

"I was teaching a class of adults last night and it was like eight moms and three dads," Mitsuaki explained while providing an update on the school's stats today. "We have a lot of moms, ladies, classes with children where there are more girls. We're a very diverse community, with children of all ethnic backgrounds. We're very popular with the Jewish and Latino communities. Sometimes there'll be twenty kids and only four or five will be Caucasian. The rest are minorities. I'm mixed. My mom is American; my father, Japanese. My wife is Brazilian. It's like the United Nations at my house! We're very accepting of all cultures and races. We're well respected in the autism community as well. I have many autistic students. Some of them are high functioning; others not at all. Some are Asperger's. We've developed a reputation because of Michael. ...We don't treat [students] differently. They come in and put a uniform on. I will slow down the pace, but we don't separate them. They do the same thing other kids do. I think that gives them a lot of confidence. They are treated as equals."

There's another person from Taido who played a very special role in my life over the years: Brendan Dumont, who is also a talented third degree black belt and now a full time Sensei too. Besides his unbelievable talents as a teacher of Taido, there are so many ways that Brendan has helped me grow as a person. Over the years, he has listened to my story ideas no matter how many times I told him the same thing over and over again. (I am told that I constantly repeat my stories, but that's another thing that's not obvious to me!) He encouraged me to try to write out my thoughts. When I was in high school, he took me hiking, out to eat, or just found time to talk to me. He's been such a special friend and has made a big difference in my life and in the lives of others over the years through his teachings and mentorship.

"In the school, we see many special-needs kids all up and down the spectrum so we do what we can to accommodate their learning style and make them feel like everybody else," Brendan said. "Sensei does not budge when it comes to certain rules. A lot of these kids have unique talents whether it be memorizing the language or counting in Japanese. I try to encourage them in that regard to give them positivity. It's a reserve of positivity to then be able to guide them in other areas. It can be hard with autistic people because they're used to their own learning style. I tutored one special-needs child for English who was born as a twin and very premature. He had different types of dyslexia, both balance and directional orientation issues. After coming to our school, he saw progress, so he asked me to be his English tutor. He eventually graduated from high school with honors. It's a blessing to be around people on the spectrum because it makes you appreciate how easy your own path has been. It's also interesting to see how people learn, cracking a code to figure out the right balance."

Taido, Uchida Sensei, Mitsuaki Sensei, Musashi Sensei, Dumont Sensei, and all the black belt students have helped me grow and have served as my second family. There is no doubt that Taido created a stronger connection between my brain and my body, helping me develop beyond my initial capabilities. They expected me to work hard, and they gave me a place where I felt like I belonged.

Eighteen years after I started Taido, I finally won a trophy in a tournament, and it did not go unnoticed by these star instructors with whom I had trained. It was a second-place finish, but I had earned it. They stood firmly with me—in tears—in front of the competitors and asked that I tell everyone how long it had taken me to earn that trophy. It was an accomplishment with true meaning.

"We have mottos," Mitsuaki said. "Never give up. Dare to do. It's not about the destination, it's about the journey. Take the path less walked. Michael believes in a lot of the sayings we teach. He believes it more than most people."

Twenty-four years later, I am a second-degree black belt. I'm grateful for the opportunity to continue my training. Taido is a place where I belong.

CHAPTER 7

Singing My Way to Greatness

**"Absorb what is useful; discard what is not;
add what is uniquely your own."**
—BRUCE LEE

IN ADDITION TO martial arts and school, a third influence in my growth and development was music. My parents were aware that music could assist brain development, so, at five years old, I was enrolled in piano classes. Once again by my side, cousins Katie and Jenny were attending the same classes.

There is no way to explain how difficult reading music was for me. I also struggled to move my fingers from one piano key to another. After reviewing my testing results while working on this book, it's quite understandable that my particular problems didn't make piano playing and reading music a realistic possibility. I wasn't like Katie and Jenny, who were playing songs very quickly. The teacher said I was unable to follow simple directions and just didn't seem interested. Not surprisingly, she told my parents that I couldn't continue the classes.

Finding someone else willing to teach me piano was another challenge. Hoping that music might make a difference, my mom kept searching for something that would work. It would take some time for the right music teacher to surface, but in the meantime, my musical talents emerged on their own. When I was 7, I attended my first funeral with my parents and someone sang "Amazing Grace." A few weeks later, I began singing it. Not only did I know the words, I could sing it on key! I had only heard the song one time, but I guess it just stuck in my head.

After that, whenever there was a family gathering, my mom would ask me to sing something. I just never understood why she wanted me to sing. It was overwhelming to be in front of everyone. Don't get me wrong, I loved to sing, but not to a gathering of people. Now that I'm beginning to understand the realities of my childhood, I recognize that my singing abilities were a big positive that she was so proud to share. I may not have been able to answer a simple question, but I was able to replicate the words and tune of a song after hearing it only once. Finding the positive, which was singing, and not just focusing on the negative, has been an ongoing theme of my life.

Eventually, when I was about 8 years old, Francesca Richards came into my life. The grandmother of two boys who were in martial arts with me, she retired to Georgia after a career of singing opera in New York. It was Mrs. Richards who overlooked my challenges and agreed to give me piano lessons once a week. But from the start, no matter how much I wanted to play the piano, it was just impossible. Reading the music and coordinating my hands on the keys was torture. She pointed to each note and patiently moved my fingers to the correct keys. It was a single movement at a time, nothing that represented a song. However, I kept going no matter how difficult it was and how little progress I was able to make.

Twice a year, Mrs. Richards had a recital for her students. Cousins Katie and Jenny were part of the classes, too, and they continued to advance. For me, the one basic song I practiced for the recital was not quite right, but my parents and the others attending always congratulated me on my efforts. Throughout those struggles, Mrs. Richards only encouraged me, and never made me feel like I was different from the others.

At the time, I wondered why I had to take piano lessons. Unlike martial arts, piano was not my passion, so my struggles made it even more difficult than martial arts. Piano felt even more difficult than learning to read! According to The American Music Therapy Association, music can be used for many things including to improve communication and promote physical rehabilitation. So, in my parents' thought process, piano lessons were just another facet of my ongoing therapy. No matter how hard those lessons were, the note-by-note effort to play the piano by first reading a note and then moving my fingers on the keyboard was helping my brain function.

In the spring of my sophomore year in high school, Mrs. Richards began giving me classical voice lessons instead of piano lessons. The songs that my former opera singing instructor taught included ones that are hundreds of years old that are traditionally taught to voice students, as well as iconic yet traditional Broadway tunes. Even though I was already able to sing, these lessons highlighted a new challenge: I had never actually read music notes. During my piano lessons, I had just been memorizing where to put my finger based on the note. My singing came from what I heard. Reading symbols was even harder than reading letters. Patiently, as always, she worked with me.

To be honest, I never became good at reading musical notes. Each time Mrs. Richards reviewed a song, she would play and sing parts of it and, although the music was right in front of me, it was her voice singing the words and notes that I absorbed. I memorized the notes I heard, not really reading them. Thus, I learned the songs in my own way.

As a voice student now, recitals were wonderful, and absolutely no comparison to those piano recitals! I could sing as good if not better than other students. I also had no problem learning to sing in Italian. I'd finally found an area where I was able to do something others could not.

LIVING LIFE IN MUSICALS
AND MARTIAL ARTS

Entering high school is an important milestone for anyone. I continued in the CommArts program at Mill Springs and had some classes with the "regular" students my freshman and sophomore years. Despite my brother and cousins attending a different school than me, I thought I had conquered a great deal of my learning challenges. The goal was to work as hard as possible and be a role model. In my mind, I was doing better than a lot of students who didn't complete assignments or were causing trouble. Never once did I think that I did not have the ability.

My freshman year of high school, I was in the play *Grease*. My role would involve participation as a cast member which included singing several songs with others. I would also sing "Blue Moon" as a solo. My grandfather had never been able to attend one of my school functions, but he was there that night. He was so thrilled to see me perform and said, "Michael, you can do anything you want in life. You just proved it tonight."

Between my black belt in karate and my singing, I had accomplished two things that many others never had. These two endeavors gave me even more confidence in my abilities. I was also meeting all of my goals in school. In my junior year, at last, I was promoted to a Level A! I was the first CommArts student in five years to be promoted to that level. It had been a lot of work, and I had been given extra responsibilities serving as a role model. I was able to maintain the Level A until I graduated. One of my teachers wrote this note about this accomplishment:

> **Michael has been a pleasure to work with over the past five years. His tireless work ethic and perseverance paid off with the reward of high marks in all his academic courses. Michael was someone who I never had to worry about not having his work or coming to class unprepared for a quiz or test. Michael had been a success outside the classroom as well. His commitment to the fine arts program has regularly netted him star roles in the theater and music programs. Perhaps my fondest memory of Michael was in his struggle to achieve Level A. When Michael first approached the community about Level A feedback, I thought he was kidding us all. In my wildest dreams, I never thought Michael would achieve such as a lofty goal, but then**

again, one shouldn't discount Michael Goodroe. He has shown everyone what dedication, commitment, and perseverance can do. I was most proud of Michael when he finally achieved Level A because this was not a mercy vote. Michael earned a Level A because he worked on every ounce of feedback he received. He is the first person that made Level A in the five years I have been at Mill Springs.

Although school work remained very difficult, my parents and I had developed our methodology to keep me on track. Any reading, from a textbook or a novel, we would do together. They would buy an extra book and we would read it out loud. Although this was a slower process, it worked for me. I was able to absorb the information, and it also strengthened my reading skills.

My dad helped me with math while my mom worked with me on written assignments. The goal was always to learn the information. It was not important how I learned it. Mom said that if I had been blind, no one would have expected me to see the words. She said that my only job was to learn the information. My homework was consistently completed, and I was prepared for each test. I could learn any information if I had assistance, but writing anything on my own remained a huge task. Constructing a sentence was like climbing a mountain some days. This is feedback from another teacher on my efforts:

I have enjoyed getting to know Michael. He is perhaps the hardest working student I have ever known. I remember when I was worried about him moving to the upper school for Algebra class, but he proved he can do whatever he sets his mind to accomplish. He will achieve whatever he sets out to do in life.

"SOMEWHERE THAT'S GREEN"

In my senior year of high school, *Little Shop of Horrors* was the final play. I had the lead role as the "Plant" with both great singing and acting opportunities. During the production, the people sitting next to my parents commented that there must have been a professional recording being used for the role of the Plant. My parents responded, "No, that's our son performing the role!"

From my standpoint, I had overcome many of my challenges. I was a high school student making life work, both on the stage and in the classroom! There was a new major hurdle, however, that was thrown into my path my junior year – the requirement to provide standardized test scores for college acceptance. Anyone planning to attend college must take the SAT and/or ACT. Standardized tests were never a positive for me, and these test results were no different.

When I took the ACT in April 2005, I earned a total score of 15, the 14th percentile, which was the lower quarter of students nationally. This was not a surprise, but there was some good news embedded in the results. In some of the subtest areas I had scored closer to the test average. For example, in the Algebra/Geometry category, I had scores in the 41st percentile of all students and in Social Studies/Science I was in the 38th percentile. To most people, this was not positive. For me, just seeing the word "average" was good news.

I also took the SAT exam – five times! My final effort resulted in my best scores and, no surprise, they were very low. I was in the 13th percentile for Reading and the 16th percentile for Math. My essay for Writing was scored at a 400.

While looking for a college that would be a good fit for me, we found several schools that specialized in educating students with learning disabilities. However, during the search process, I received information about applying to college based on my ability to sing classical music. It turns out that my singing opened doors that could not have been imagined, even with my educational challenges. I auditioned at three colleges and sang "Gia Il Sole Dal Gange," by Alessandro Scarlatti, an Italian song from the 17th century, and "Now Sleeps the Crimson Petal," by Roger Quilter.

Despite my daring song choices and the fact that I successfully pulled them off, one school immediately realized I didn't have the ability to apply the technical theory of music, so it was a "no" from them. However, I auditioned at two other colleges and both were interested in me joining their programs. This was an exciting time as I had the opportunity to attend college! I chose the University of West Georgia (UWG), which was located about ninety miles from home. The excitement was tempered when I was notified that my SAT scores were an issue to my admission.

Based on my SAT scores, a "presidential exception" was required as part of my admission. Dr. Kevin Hibbard, the dean of the Music Department, was my advocate and requested them to consider the exception for admission. The admission director looked at my records and told my mom that I would last one semester "even if I got in." As expected, Mom told him not to count me out.

While Dr. Hibbard had passionately advocated for me to be accepted, he didn't know at the time that I was autistic. In his own words: "Sometimes you don't realize you made a difference until someone contacts you later or quotes something you said that you didn't remember saying at all. You have to be careful because even the slightest comment can be remembered. We have students we admit as music majors, but sometimes they don't get admitted to the university. In Michael's case, I called the director of admissions. He said Michael's scores were too low, but he told me about the presidential exception, which required a letter detailing what impact this person would have on the program and why, in my opinion, this person should be admitted. I've only done three or four and Michael's was the first, and this is my 28th year here, 13th year as chair of the Music Department. Michael's auditions were performed in front of me acting as choir director and the opera director, and we both thought he would make a positive impact on our program. I stated this in the letter, adding that he would have an immediate impact on the quality of the choir, the sound, and that's all I remember saying. Next thing I knew, he was admitted! When I wrote that letter, I didn't know he was autistic, not that it would have mattered."

Once all of the required puzzle pieces were in place, the exception was granted. Singing was my ticket into college, and against all odds, I had the opportunity of a lifetime. The dean of the Music Department did something wonderful for me by looking beyond my disability and my SAT scores!

Finishing my senior year of high school having been accepted into a regular university was the most fantastic time of my life. My parents were ecstatic. My graduation was like something out of a movie for all of us. There was so much to celebrate. Not only was I graduating from high school; I had a future!

The principal of CommArts, Kay Morrison, had known me for six years by that point. She wrote a letter to my parents, summarizing my past five years of progress.

We have been on an amazing journey...the journey that has brought us to the point where Michael has been accepted to several colleges. How proud we all are! Sometimes that road was bumpy for Michael, but he kept trying. Michael often had to work three times as hard as other students to reach his goals, but he never, never gave up. I don't think that any student at Mill Springs has ever worked as hard to get to Level A. Every week Michael would go up for feedback, and every week we saw him work on those issues of social interaction...issues that didn't come easily to Michael. He kept plodding along, heading towards his goal and never looking back or making excuses. Like the turtle, he got there slowly, but he got there as a solid Level A. The greatest lesson that we have learned from Michael is that you can never, ever, underestimate the abilities of any person. When I worked with Michael on one of our first festivals (featuring Japan), I was startled when Michael memorized the Japanese song we were studying in just one day...all in Japanese. At that moment, I realized that we were not dealing with an ordinary student. That was the first of many academic challenges that Michael would not only meet, but excel in. No one can ever tell me that the student in CommArts can't handle anything they set their minds to, and Michael is our greatest example of that.

When we put Michael in all upper classes, he was consistently earning A's, which did not surprise us that had grown to know him. I want to follow Michael's progress in life because I know he will continue to accomplish his life goals, and make us all so proud.

Another teacher wrote a few words on what he thought had made a difference. Most importantly, what I had been able to accomplish made him think differently about his expectations for other students. This is what my mom kept trying to tell others; she saw more in me than just what the testing showed.

In the past six years, Michael has taught me about the power of determination, focus and a positive attitude. These are attributes that he has shown on his journey. Michael's character and particularly his willingness to take on challenges have inspired me to look for more opportunities for our students so that they can develop their character.

There was a similar message from another teacher. She credited my parents for expecting me to continue to reach new goals. Again, it's clear that my success was a nice surprise and one that should help others think positively about their potential.

I have admired the way that Michael's parents have always supported but also expected Michael to continue to grow and reach new goals. This is an example that each of us has learned from. Michael has taught us so much more than we have taught him.

Other teachers wrote positive comments, but some have very special meaning to me, like this one, which refers to a Samurai warrior, an iconic figure that I researched and presented as part of my high school curriculum:

Michael, in the past forty years, I guess I have taught almost 5,000 students. I have forgotten the names and faces of many, if

not most of them. But you will always be in the group of students I will never forget. Keep pushing forward. Like a great Samurai warrior, you have sliced away any doubts about how intelligent and talented you are. Always believe in yourself and follow your dreams.

Finally, when I gave my speech at graduation, I was introduced to the audience with the following words:

If you looked up "go-getter" in the dictionary, it would have a picture of Michael Goodroe. But it wouldn't be any old picture—it would be one of Michael smiling, because that is who he is. Whether it's school work, martial arts, drama, or singing, Michael works hard. He really goes after it, reaching for his goal without complaint and without delay. Give him a goal and he starts working toward succeeding. Michael describes himself as "just a normal guy," but he is not normal. He has proved he is exceptional. For anyone that has watched Michael perform, you will understand how much he will be missed. As he graduates, we realize that we only have one more time to say, ladies and gentlemen…here is Michael Goodroe.

Using no notes, I gave my graduation speech. I wasn't nervous. I was grateful for the opportunity. When I finished my speech, I sang "The Impossible Dream," by Mitch Leigh. When I received my diploma, I stopped and did a cartwheel. Of course, the idea had come from Mitsuaki Sensei. Both he and Brendan Sensei were there to celebrate with me. Once, I would not have had the balance and coordination to do this.

The headmaster of Mill Springs recalls: "While Michael didn't have an even profile, he had some strengths. He didn't present them very well, but he had them. One way they were demonstrated, interestingly enough, for somebody who would not respond well socially or communicate when he was younger, was when he got involved with drama, theatre, and singing. It was fascinating to watch him grow so quickly or communicate as another character. That helped him augment the strengths he had on the achievement side. He had that same kind of drive in martial arts. You wouldn't know he was at such a high level of martial arts. He didn't talk about it or test it on the playground. He might do a cartwheel off the stage. Otherwise, he was quietly determined."

Who knew a high school graduation ceremony could be so exciting? No wonder I thought I had no significant problems.

CHAPTER 8

Opportunity Does
Not Mean It Is Easy

"To hell with circumstances; I create opportunities."
—BRUCE LEE

THE SUMMER PASSED quickly and I was both very nervous and excited about college. I had never been on my own, and I had never
been anywhere by myself. My mom had decided that my transition to
college needed some extra steps, just like everything else I had done
in life. She checked into a hotel room near UWG to make sure the
first week was not too overwhelming for me.

It was finally time for my first big collegiate step – moving into the
freshman dorm. I'll never forget seeing all those other students with
their families. What a change from my small school where I knew
everyone. Both my parents and I were very nervous even though they
kept assuring me that everything was going to be all right. We'd only
been in the dorm for five minutes when the police took away three
students in handcuffs. The rumor was that they'd been selling drugs.
This definitely was a different world than I had ever seen!

Although the rooms housed two students, I didn't have a roommate. The advisor who assisted disability students thought that, with
my diagnosis, having to share a room would make it difficult for me
to study and sleep and would just be an added stress. My parents and
I agreed.

We concentrated on getting the room to feel like it was mine. I had my own small refrigerator and a television. Without a roommate, there was plenty of room. The bathrooms were down the hall, and I soon realized that I had to adjust to facilities that were usually in terrible condition since this was the male dorm. While I pondered all this, my mom was more concerned with the emotional component. I had no idea at the time, but she was worried that I knew no one at UWG, a problem since making friends was harder for me than other students. She was also very concerned about how others would treat me.

The day after move-in, classes began, but my first one didn't start until late morning. I have never been great at sleeping and that first night was quite difficult. My mom picked me up to take me to IHOP for breakfast. Usually both of us love pancakes but neither of us could eat a bite of our food. She was as nervous as I was even though she didn't want to admit it at the time.

During the summer, I had met with the counselor from disability services, and she had reviewed the list of accommodations that had been outlined from my testing in the eighth grade. She had written a form letter for me to give each of my professors. She said it was up to me to work with each one of them so that they understood what I needed. This is what the accommodation letter said about how my disability affected me:

How the Disability Affects Student in Class or On Campus:

1. **His speed of processing is slower than most; it takes extra time for him to absorb what is being seen or what is being read.**
2. **His cursive handwriting is very slow and difficult to read.**
3. **The mechanics of written composition—spelling, punctuation, sentence structure—is a major area of disability.**
4. **Putting his own ideas into written words is difficult for him. Speaking his ideas is much easier.**
5. **His conversation may be somewhat stiff and literal.**
6. **The math disability lies in the areas of math reasoning and computation. This is an especially difficult area for Michael.**

Strengths and Additional Resources:

1. He has an understanding and acceptance of his disabilities and social differences.
2. He expresses his ideas best using a laptop computer.
3. He is well organized.
4. He is accomplished in vocal music, karate.

Required Classroom Accommodations to Aid Student in Reaching Standards and Requirements of Courses:

1. He is entitled to have up to double time on all tests or timed in-class assignments, if he asks in advance, including the Regents Test.
2. He is entitled to take tests in a quiet, non-distracting area.
3. He is entitled to tape record lectures.
4. He is entitled to type rather than handwrite tests or essays.
5. He is entitled to record or dictate to a scribe his response to essay questions.

This was Fall of 2006, and the process for accommodations was newer and less formalized than it is now. Most of my professors had never had any type of request for accommodations and didn't know how to handle it. Many were very helpful; others were not. Just having someone willing to share their notes with me was difficult to achieve. Often, I found myself reminding the person who had volunteered, sometimes the notes were not complete, and there were times when I received no notes at all.

I recently reviewed the current UWG website and was amazed at the extensive amount of information about accommodations available now compared to ten years ago when I started college. Not only is there a specific form to help someone with an autism spectrum disorder. There are now "note taker guidelines" set up, which makes the process less difficult. A student has to ability to keep their request confidential so no one knows who's requesting the accommodation.

The note takers are paid a stipend and also receive early registration for the following semester. (What a great benefit for sharing notes.) They can also request that their notes be typed and returned within twenty-four hours.

A STUDY IN EXTREME STUDY TECHNIQUES

Due to my low SAT scores, I was required to take the collegiate placement examination to determine which English and Math classes I needed. I scored two points lower than required on English so was placed in the basic composition course. I was also required to take a class to improve my reading. My parents explained why this was a much better way to start my college experience. They knew that both these classes were essential to improving my chances of succeeding. My first semester, therefore, consisted of the Reading and English classes and a variety of music classes including Music Theory, Aural Skills, Applied Voice, Concert Choir, and a Music Lab.

By the end of the first week of school, my appetite had returned. Mom, who'd been staying at a nearby hotel, went home, so I would be on my own the following week. I attended classes and checked in with my parents after each one so we could make sure all was going well. By the end of the week, some other freshmen in the dorm had noticed me. To make a long story short, their intentions were to pull a prank on me. They managed to convince me that there was an anime (Japanese comic book) club on campus, and that they were having a meeting that night, so I set out to join the club. There was no club. It worried my mom, so she asked that I keep them updated when I was going to do something they didn't know was on the schedule. Each weekend, I would return home to study with my parents, who knew that my success was dependent on a disciplined approach to studying, now more than ever before. Although I had a driver's license by this time (it took me three times to pass the driver's written test), someone would come to retrieve me for our weekend study marathon.

My mother recalls: "When Michael got to college, it was extraordinary what we had to do to help him learn. The amount of time he put in every week, it was something I don't think anybody would do. On Fridays, one of us would drive to get him. He would drive short distances, but we thought it was too stressful for him to drive any further. Every moment from the time he got home until Sunday, we would read every page in every book. Mike and Michael would do the reading and I would make study guides and practice tests on every subject he had. It was an extraordinary amount of work. Our other son probably got the short end of the stick. We never scheduled anything else during this time. We were fine with it because we were so grateful he had the opportunity. So grateful. He has always been willing to work hard."

During the school week, I would scan any notes from classes I had received and send them to my mother. I had purchased two books for each class so my parents would have one too. By the time I arrived home each weekend, my mom had made study guides and had filled in any holes in my notes from class. My dad would read each page of every assignment with me. He would read a page out loud and then I would read the next page. This allowed me to absorb the information. My reading and comprehension skills became stronger and stronger.

When we would take a break, there were practice tests for me to take that my mom had designed. By the time I returned to school late on Sundays, I had a plan for the week. We went over each syllabus so that I would use my time wisely at school each week. It was an extremely disciplined effort for all three of us. There was almost no free time, but my parents kept reminding me what a great opportunity this was for me.

Anyone who thinks that music is an easy college major is wrong. Music theory was like a foreign language to me. And in the labs, I had to identify individual notes played on tape. Hearing a note by itself made no sense to me, and I couldn't comprehend what I was hearing. It certainly didn't sound like music to me! I tried everything, but it became clear that I could *not* be a music major. However, I could still participate in the concert choir.

Many people are lost when they start college. They have no place where they belong. For me, I had the chorus group, which was wonderful for me. I looked forward to seeing everyone at class, and each day I would arrive early so I could visit with the other students before we got started.

Our first concert was the week before Thanksgiving. My family came to campus early to see me before the concert started. I had a surprise for them but didn't say a word about it before the performance. Later, I was backstage when my family, already seated, saw the printed program for the first time. There was only one solo performance for the night and it belonged to me: an African-themed song titled "Shosholoza." The word "shoshloza" means to move forward or to strive for something. It was the perfect song for me to sing! For my parents, it was one of the best surprises ever. Instead of me being surrounded by more challenges, I had found my way to be part of something positive. In my tuxedo, singing a wonderful song and an unexpected solo, I stood out in a good way. It was a special night and one that none of us will ever forget.

My mother still beams at the memory. "I was driving to the college feeling so much happiness in my heart. Michael was part of a college activity. He was part of a group. No one was thinking about his disability. I can still see him walking toward me in his tuxedo with a big smile. It was a moment that is etched in my mind. When I looked at the program and saw his name next to the solo, I felt tears running down my cheeks. That night was like a dream come true."

PERSUASIONS OF THE FITTEST

I completed all of my first semester classes except Aural Skills, a one-hour credit course which I had dropped. I made B's in both Reading and English. My only C was in Music Theory. I had earned 16 credits and had a GPA of 2.66. This was an amazing feeling! One semester down and not a bad GPA for someone who was predicted not to make it at all.

There were plenty of general electives to take so I didn't decide my new major until the end of my freshman year. My second semester classes included: Public Speaking, Introduction to Mass Communications, English, History of Jazz, Rock and Pop Music and Concert Choir. When I received the syllabuses at the beginning of that second semester, I sensed it would be an overwhelming challenge. The first thing I did in each class was meet with the professors to share my list of accommodations. After I gave it to my Public Speaking professor, she asked me if I thought I should find another class that might be a better fit for me. She believed I would have a very tough time in her class because of my autism. I told her that I didn't have a problem speaking in front of people and that I'd been in plays at school and had also spoken at my high school graduation. Thankfully, I was able to take the class and dispel any doubts she may have had!

There were a lot of assignments in that public speaking class, and I received positive feedback on all of them. The final project assigned was to present a persuasive speech. The guidelines stated that a student should pick a topic where others may not share your same opinion, with the goal of persuading them that your point of view is correct. My mom suggested that I try to convince my audience that people with autism and learning disabilities have even more ability to achieve success in college than those who easily succeeded in high school.

In order to prepare for the presentation, there was a great deal of research that had to be done. First, I had to research autism, which I did, but I have to admit that it was hard for me to see myself in the words that describe the condition. For example, people with autism don't read social ques. Therefore, if someone doesn't want me to tell them my stories anymore, I don't see that they're giving me that signal. I just keep talking. So, what I see happening is not always what others may see.

The premise for my speech was simple: Someone who did well in high school with little or no effort may not succeed in college. My parents had shared so many stories with me of students with academic strengths who had dropped out of college. Success occurs when someone is willing to work hard and show up consistently. That's been such an important lesson in my life. I received my first A in college in Public Speaking and the professor said that she had been very surprised by my ability to speak in front of a group.

The premise of my speech actually proved to be true in our extended family. Two of my cousins, Katie (who I have mentioned before and Meredith were both born around the same time I was. Both of my cousins had been excellent, talented students throughout high school and both had been accepted at prestigious colleges. Well, it turned out that both dropped out of college during their second semesters. It's an important lesson in life, and one that made me appreciate, once again, the story of *The Tortoise and Hare*, which also held special meaning for me relating to my success in martial arts. Success is based on many factors, but showing up and working hard are monumental. I was the one who had earned credits for two semesters in college. It was the first time ever that I was ahead in the race. Of course, it's also important to remember that everyone has their own unique path to take, and my cousins have found their own.

My public speaking class gave me more assurance in my abilities. I had been in plays in school and had also done some speaking at high school events, but to achieve an A in a college course on speaking increased my confidence tremendously. Also, the topic of my final project required me to learn more about autism. It was such a positive way for me to become informed about the challenges that I had not allowed to define me.

Finishing my second semester, I had all B's except for a C in English. This gave me a total of 40 hours earned for the first two semesters and a GPA of 3.07. My parents had worked with me through each step. The amount of work was enormous, but my reading and comprehension skills were growing so much stronger. It made me realize that I could take on the challenge of a history major which required a tremendous amount of reading. I had always enjoyed studying history in high school. My dad, who loves to joke, said that he never knew *he* wanted to study history!

I also had found that I could live on my own. Each Sunday evening, I would go to the grocery store and buy food for the week. I would eat one meal a day at a campus fast food restaurant and prepare the other two meals myself. I didn't actually cook anything, but made sandwiches and other things that were easy to handle. I did this to make sure I wasn't eating too many calories. There are lots of things that I like to eat, and I knew I'd gain too much weight if I wasn't careful.

My mom recalled a telephone call she received my freshman year from one of the professors on campus. She was worried until she realized that he was asking her for assistance. He told her that he didn't have me in a class, but a friend of his had told him about me. It turned out that the professor had a son with my same diagnosis. He asked if she would meet with his wife and him to share some thoughts on how to prepare their son for high school. Mom said that this gave her assurance that I was on a positive track overall.

While I was looking forward to taking a break from school all summer, my parents convinced me to take one class. It was an accelerated six-week class, which meant that it was like taking two classes. I chose American Government and made an A. The next six weeks, I enjoyed my time off and attended karate as much as I could. I had missed Taido a lot. It was great to be back, and I had a lot to celebrate after completing my first year of college!

DESIGNED TO BE INCOGNITO

My sophomore year started with a change in my living situation. I was assigned to a small apartment on campus with three other male students. Each of us had a tiny private bedroom with a shared kitchen. I stayed in my room except when I was making myself something to eat. It was just more comfortable for me to be in my own space. If I saw any of my roommates, I would say hi, but there were many days I saw no one. I liked early classes, and my roommates were asleep when I was up in the morning. We were on opposite schedules, so, overall, there were no issues. The same can be said about my social life in college, which mainly consisted of seeing people in my classes. I never was invited to a party or out to dinner with anyone. I looked forward to going to class and was usually one of the first ones waiting for it to start. I understand that people with autism have difficulty with socialization skills. It's just hard to explain because I never figured out what to do differently, but I was content being in college and moving ahead with my life.

My Fall classes were very intense. I was taking Astronomy with a lab, English II, World History, Quantitative Reasoning and Choir. Once again, my parents helped me organize and study. Somehow, I was able to obtain a B in English but only had a C in my history class. My GPA for the semester was 2.71. One more semester down, and it was now time to declare a major and a minor. Even though my history class had been quite challenging, I declared history as my major and chose theatre as my minor.

By the end of Fall semester my junior year, my grade point average was above of a 3.0 and it stayed there for the rest of college. This was significant because I was then considered a HOPE scholar for the state of Georgia. The HOPE scholarship paid tuition at public colleges for students with a GPA of 3.0 and above. Not only was I making it through college, I was on a scholarship offered to any in-state student who maintained an average above 3.0. I had an academic scholarship! There are no words to express how proud my parents were.

There was only one significant incident that occurred during my third year. I had signed up for an Asian history class, which I was very interested in because of my love for martial arts. The professor told me I couldn't attend his class after I gave him my accommodation sheet the first day. I was very upset and concerned that I had done something wrong. I've always wanted to be compliant. I think I may have been too excited about the class and shown it by asking too many questions.

It was the only time that my mom demanded a meeting with the university. She was livid, and I was the one that had to ask her to calm down. In the end, I didn't get back in the class because the professor had tenure, which basically means he can do whatever he wants to. The people from the university, including the chairman of the History Department, apologized for what had happened. Overall, my parents and I had nothing but positive things to say about UWG and didn't see the actions of one person as a reflection of all the good that had occurred. It was important to concentrate on all the positive things that were happening to me and not the one thing that had been a problem.

By my third year, I was unable to coordinate my class schedule with choir, so I could no longer take it. I really missed it because choir was a place where I had something in common with my classmates. My weeks were very busy with school work, but I wanted to do other things, too. It's no surprise that it was hard to find a place where I fit in. A new gym had been built on campus and since I wasn't attending karate on a regular basis, I joined and signed up for someone to help me work out. It was great. I developed more muscle tone, and it was a nice break from my school work. My parents noted that I had found this opportunity on my own – another sign that I was thriving.

I also enjoyed my theatre classes which, while providing a degree of structure, were also very interactive, just like choir had been. This was great for me, and I looked forward to being with the other students. One of the requirements for theatre was working on sets, manual labor which required using hammers, screwdrivers and other equipment. This didn't come easily to me, but my required four semesters of doing it helped me develop many new skills.

My fourth year in college, I had to move to an apartment off campus – another big step. It was the first time I had a car at school, which allowed me to venture off campus by myself. I would sometimes eat at different restaurants around town, and I'd also go to the local comic store. It turned out that it was owned by one of the history professors, and his mom worked there most days. Because of the added stress of driving in very heavy traffic and long distances, my family still drove me back and forth for weekend study sessions.

I continued to take a class or two each summer semester so I was able to graduate in five years. Throughout my entire time at college, I had never missed a class, and I had never been late for a class. This is another important lesson. Sometimes just showing up is a bigger step toward success than people realize.

History turned out to be a wonderful major for me. I enjoyed the subject matter and found the lectures gratifying. For the papers that had to be written, my mother would help me gather the information from the library and then we worked together to get everything in the right format. I knew the information, but I had a lot of difficulty with the grammar and structure required to write a paper. This has not changed, and she's helped me with this book also. But all in all, I must have been doing something right. My final year, I was nominated by my professors for the Phi Alpha Theta International Honor Society in History. At the induction, my parents were even more proud when they found that only one other student had been nominated for this honor.

In what seemed like no time at all, I was graduating. For most everyone who graduates from college, it's a bittersweet time. I was glad to take a break from the studying, but I missed the college environment. All in all, I'm so glad that my parents pushed me to take the more challenging path of pursuing a higher education.

Dr. Hibbard, my greatest advocate for entry into college besides my parents, recalls: "Sometimes barriers can be broken instead of worked around. As an educator, you see so many students at a critical time in their lives and watch how they deal with such obstacles. Some are successful and some are not. As a counselor for students, I see some of them make bad choices. But look at Michael! He's a great kid, but some thought there was no way he'd get a degree and then low and behold, he's on the graduation list. He was talented and brilliant in certain ways. The students would congregate in the hallway before rehearsal, and it would be like he was holding court, quoting movies and in character. It was amazing how talented he was at that. He was slow to learn music but once he learned through so many hearings, he contributed greatly because his voice was so good."

Hibbard adds a tip for all college freshmen: "Don't give up. Keep trying different things you can be successful at and that you enjoy. Michael had done music in high school and had achieved success; that's what he enjoyed. I was glad that he continued in the choir and was disappointed when he stopped, but he was experiencing other things, which I support. Some students come to university and all they do is take classes. They don't get involved with organizations or performing arts, student government or any myriad of opportunities there are out there. It's a time of your life when you should experience as much as possible."

CHAPTER 9

Degree in Grit

"The future looks extremely bright indeed, with lots of possibilities ahead—big possibilities. Like the song says, 'We've just begun'."
—BRUCE LEE

COMPLETING COLLEGE WAS a great feeling! I believe I'm like a lot of college graduates; that elation doesn't last long. In 2011, the job market was very tight even for people without autism. Unfortunately, someone with autism isn't going to be high on the list as a competitive applicant. I applied for entry-level jobs like crazy. I never even had an interview. It was tough because I had thought that the reason I went to college was so I could get a job.

Once again, family helped out. My mom's brother, Uncle Richard, gave me a job at his small medical billing company. I would start out doing odd jobs. The office was about a 50-minute drive from where I lived. Although the people were nice, there were only five of them, and they were all much older than me. It made me miss college a lot. I would refer to my job as a "dead end." Somebody finally pointed out that even if I thought that, it wasn't the type of attitude you should voice at work. Obviously, understanding *not* to verbalize an honest thought doesn't fit in within the parameters of autism.

There was one situation that occurred which demonstrates the concrete thinking of my brain. Uncle Richard had said I was welcome to indulge in any snack food stocked at the office. One day, I packed up a couple of candy bars and chips to bring home. He then explained to me that the food in question was for the office, and he didn't think when he said "take whatever you want" that I would take his words so literally. It's still a challenge for me to see multiple or subtle meanings in some words.

SUMMONING MY SUPERHERO

Over time, my responsibilities at work have grown. I enter data and complete different jobs whenever needed. The work wasn't difficult, and I wanted to do more, so my mom suggested that I take a medical billing and coding class. At the end of the class, you can attempt to become certified, which makes you more attractive as a hire.

Once again, Mom and Dad were helping me study. It was one of the most challenging subjects I've tried to learn. I was able to learn the definitions, but the rules for the actual medical coding were like a foreign language. However, I felt much better when my mom tried to take the practice tests and she failed too! I took the 6-week class twice and didn't pass the exam, so medical billing and coding would not be a profession for me. However, I did learn a lot of new information.

After college, I was able to return to Taido martial arts classes three to four times each week. The workouts were great, being around my friends there even better, and my job was fine, but I was anxious to work on something that I was passionate about. I had always loved comic books and wanted to write my own series. For a long time, I have been fascinated with ninjas. In my mind, I could see two ninjas from competing clans in a comic book story line. This was my first independent project; this was my vision. But a comic book requires exceptional art, and I am definitely not an artist. I had outlined each character in my mind when I was working on the script. After my Taido workouts, I always talked about things I was doing, and one day I mentioned my comic book idea. One of the new black belt students, Jennifer, was home from college and she was an artist. I asked if I could hire her to do the artwork for my comic book. We started meeting once a week to go over my vision of the characters, and Jennifer brought them to life. We worked all summer, and the comic book was progressing. There was a delay in the next step because Jennifer returned to college and was too busy with schoolwork to dedicate any time to my project. Over her breaks and throughout the next summer, we worked. Finally, the comic book was finished! I had one hundred copies printed. It was exciting, but I also realized how much work goes into the development of comic books.

Meanwhile, I decided to try another creative venture. I had always been a fan of obscure martial arts movies. I decided to review a movie each month and post to YouTube. This would require me to learn how to clip portions of a movie and insert my own taped reviews. With no assistance, I was able to develop a series called *The Martial Arts Guy*. For the past three years, I have reviewed movies and posted to YouTube. Several of my reviews have received enough views to generate advertising. I learned a lot from the experience and realized that I need to keep working on things like this.

Since college, I've also continued my singing at different events including charity functions and weddings. Twice, I had the opportunity to perform the National Anthem at the Autism Speaks Walk in Georgia, which are attended by thousands of people. Some are amazed at my ability to sing in front of large groups but as long as I know in advance, I don't have a problem. I actually love performing!

All this being said, I knew I needed a "next step" after graduating from college. I wanted to start a comic book company, but my parents pointed out that even though I loved comic books, I didn't know anything about running a company. They suggested that I enroll in a Master's in Business Administration program to get a better understanding of what it takes to start and grow a business.

Of course, it was important to find a graduate program that would be a good fit for me. I wanted to have interaction with classmates, so that ruled out the online class route. I also needed a program that wouldn't determine my eligibility using my scores on the Graduate Management Admission Test (GMAT). I found a program and applied.

They required applicants to take the GMAT exam, but they didn't list a specific score that needed to be obtained. I took the test. Based on my previous testing experience, my parents and I decided not to even check my scores. It had never been good news in the past, and we didn't want to feel discouraged if my scores weren't good.

A few weeks later, I received an acceptance letter from the program at Reinhardt University.

Starting something new has always caused me to feel anxious. There were only eight students in the program, all much older than me and all with years of experience in the job market. Some of their positions, such as vice president of a bank and electrical engineer, were very impressive. Everyone was asked to share their background and goal for the class. I shared my background, said I wanted to start a comic book company, and stated that I was hoping the program would increase my knowledge of what that would take and help me see if this was something I wanted to try. I also told them I had autism.

Classes were one night a week with lots of work to be accomplished in between. My parents and I used the same study routine we'd used before. The information wasn't similar to any of the classes I had taken in college. One of the first books assigned was a detailed case study of how Steve Jobs utilized his presentation skills to make Apple successful. The description of his presentations jumped off the page and into my head. The MBA program required lots of presentations so I worked constantly to emulate what I had learned about successful ones.

Every class over the 18-month program was related to the real or pretend company that each student chose. This was the perfect way for me to relate the information to a comic book company. For every class, such as marketing, human resources, financial, strategic, and so on, I used my pretend company, White Tiger Comics, to model my business. I learned so much in this program, and it introduced me to the realities of business.

Several semesters into the program, a surprise package was delivered to my home – an edible fruit arrangement addressed to me. My mom was so curious as to why I received this. When I told her that one of my classmates was trying to recruit me to be her partner on a project, she looked surprised. It turned out that I was viewed as having strong presentation skills, and this group needed someone to do the presentation since it was a significant part of the grade. My parents were very excited, although at the time I didn't appreciate why. After learning more about my background while writing this book, I can now understand the reason this news brought them such joy. I have some talents that emerged in spite of my deficits.

"Sometimes autism is viewed as a problem," said Dr. Katherine Hyatt, associate professor and dean of the McCamish School of Business. She taught the first and last class of the program that I enrolled in. "Some people have negative connotations. What strikes me about Michael is that he was incredibly smart and well-prepared and, even though he would get nervous that he might stutter or repeat himself, I don't think autism is something that limits someone. His energy and charisma and brilliance allowed him to show the other students the knowledge and abilities that he possesses. It was a pleasure to see him progress and earn the respect of his classmates. He was one of the students that shined. Other professors would agree that he stands out. He was one of the favorites just because he was so well-prepared and well-read."

Relevant to my story, Dr. Hyatt is also a fan of Angela Duckworth's book, *Grit: The Power of Passion and Perseverance* in which the author talks about how she was often told by her dad, a scientist, that she was not that smart. Grit is a form of intellectual ability, so Duckworth created a grit scale. Dr. Hyatt points to the example on that scale of overcoming setbacks to conquer an important challenge. She's even done research on students, trying to figure out what makes them persevere, and which ones are the least likely, and most likely, to drop out. As evidenced by the book's results and my own story, it's not necessarily the ones with the highest GPA that persevere.

Dr. Hyatt tells me that she still has the White Tiger Comics T-shirt and comic book that accompanied my presentation in her first class. She called the presentation "probably by far the best presentation any of the students had done." Of course, I felt deeply encouraged to challenge myself even further.

As such, while I was working and attending the MBA program, I was asked to give the

Keynote speech at an autism education event hosted by Jacksonville State University. This was the first time I was in the keynote position, and I was excited to have the opportunity. After my speech, several people asked if I had written a book. I realized that when I completed my MBA, the next step would be this book.

CHAPTER 10

The Ultimate Test

"I fear not the man who has practiced 10,000 kicks once, but I fear the man who has practiced one kick 10,000 times."
—BRUCE LEE

AS I'VE SAID, when I began a detailed review of my records, I was overwhelmed by my own history. I had no idea the many obstacles that had been navigated over the years. As a history major, I learned that events are not one dimensional but I never thought it applied to the way I saw myself. In other words, my view of my own journey had not been a complete picture. But as I dug deeper into my story, organizing it for this book by events, milestones, setbacks and successes, my goal to provide meaningful information to others was being realized. There was also an unexpected benefit to this effort. In understanding more about myself, I am able to continue to grow and develop. In particular, I see my social skills and communication challenges with more clarity. The more I understand, the more I am able to set new goals for improvement. And I also see with greater clarity how my story came together.

FAMILY FIRST

Family has supported me every step of my life. Yes, that's what family's for, but it becomes even more essential when dealing with life's challenges. From the time I was diagnosed, both of my parents supported me – that, they've always done – but each played their own unique role in my life, bringing their specific strengths into play.

My dad has always made my life seem like any other child's. He didn't want to focus on the things my mom did. Instead, Dad did all the things that a father can do with their child. Even now, we travel together, attend Taido karate, sing together and just experience the joys of father and son as a whole. Anything that I've needed help accomplishing, my dad has been and will be there for me.

My mom used her talents and expertise to define and push onto the next step. She set the goals and found ways to go around the obstacles. Mom was the one who took my negative diagnosis and helped me push through the brick wall it represented, even if it sometimes meant only modest progress. She has always encouraged me to set new goals and chase my dreams.

My parents represent the yin and yang of my success, embodying the Chinese philosophy of two opposites sharing complementary efforts. Each of them has brought a different type of strength to my life which has allowed me to flourish. Both have encouraged me to keep going in the face of adversity and to stay positive.

Some people may say things like, "But I love my child just the way he is," as if my parents pushed me because they didn't love me for who I was. In reality it's just the opposite. They saw in me potential that others did not see. They saw the side of me that only parents know about their own children, so I'm very glad they kept looking for a path for me so I would have opportunities. They realized that I could learn, but I needed to use different methods in order to succeed. There was a focus on the positive and not just the negative.

My brother, Nathan, also played a significant part in my success story. He was born shortly after I was diagnosed when I was five years old. Of course, Nathan and I are very different people. Growing up, he was very talented and smart. I wanted to be the stereotypical big brother who takes care of their younger sibling. Now, I realize that I was just the opposite. Nathan has always been supportive of me, and has always included me in his life. I also know that the extra time my parents spent with me represented time taken away from Nathan. He never complained.

Looking back at everything with a different perspective after delving into my past, I recognize with greater clarity Nathan's steadfast love for me, even when he was just a young toddler. My fascination with comic books and their pictures that have always come to life for me was obvious to anyone who knew me. A home video, taken when I was seven and Nathan was just two, shows him finding a comic book that Santa had left me. Nathan was so excited and exclaimed, "Michael, look! A comic book!" I was looking at several other presents, and it's obvious I was unable to process Nathan's words at the time, so I didn't respond. It's sad to see my lack of reaction to Nathan's excitement, but as I read my testing results, I'm able to understand more about my auditory processing problem. Most other children would have shown an immediate reaction to something they loved so much. Nathan certainly knew that it was a special gift that should have been exciting to me. Examples of my brother's love and support have never wavered.

Many years later, on a weekday when Nathan was away at college, I was scheduled to speak at the Centers for Disease Control at their autism event—a considerable honor. It was the first time I would speak at such a high-profile event. Nathan had a big exam the next day, but he drove all the way to Atlanta to be there with me. I was so nervous before the event started, and it was Nathan who paced the back of the room with me, giving me so much encouragement. He knew how to keep me calm. He was so proud of me and said it was a night that he would never forget.

When I tell people that we never fought, they don't believe me. But it's true. I guess I found my own way to handle things. Take the television incident, a legendary story that remains a family favorite. I was watching television, but Nathan wanted to see something else. He won and I was angry but didn't say a thing to him – another example of my nonverbal behavior. Mom was in the other room and I asked her for a magic marker. Eventually I brought the marker back to her and said, "I crossed Nathan out of the family." She asked me what I meant. I spoke no words, but instead grabbed her hand and led her around the house to show her all of the pictures of Nathan. I had placed a large "X" over him in each one, including a canvas portrait that was done when he was a only few weeks old. My actions here were a great example of my concrete mind. Deciding to cross out all the pictures of my television-controlling brother, I had "borrowed" the symbol of a ghost with an "X" across it from the movie *Ghostbusters*. How's that for the power of media?

Having Nathan as a brother helped me so much because he treated me like I was just his brother. He never made me feel bad about who I was. Nathan graduated from Clemson University with a bachelor's degree in Electrical Engineering just like my dad. He's now married to Carly, who is smart, pretty and kind. I was worried about losing Nathan, but instead I'm so glad to have Carly as my sister-in-law.

My immediate and extended family have been so instrumental in helping me achieve my success, but I was also blessed with nannies who cared for me and my two cousins, Jenny and Katie. They became, and even after thirty years remain an important part of my extended family. They now take care of my cousins' two children! Olga is almost 100 years old and more active than you can imagine. Giga is in her mid-seventies, and she is both family and a great friend to me. Since my parents worked in opposite directions from my school, she would drive me the very long distance every morning and afternoon. My difficult days were always met by Giga who would make me feel better about things.

Since I was often nonverbal, Giga would sometimes "test" me to see if I was paying attention. For example, driving to school, she would deliberately miss a turn to see what I would do. I was always paying attention. I would speak up. Little did I know that she was just confirming what she believed – that I was fine.

Each and every time I succeeded at something, there were other people who played a part in my success and who deserve a great deal of the credit. Yes, I have a wonderful family, but I've also been blessed by the many "heroes" that entered my life. What a difference these people have made! There are many special people in this world, and my story shows how someone can affect someone else's life. I hope I've inspired others to make a difference.

TAKE ADVANTAGES

As we were working on this book, I became very concerned about many of the advantages I've had in life compared to others. I told my mom that anyone could be successful with as much love and support from others as I've had. In addition, my parents had the resources to send me to a private school. Of course, there was only one school that would even consider me so resources didn't make a difference in finding that school. My mom explained that even though I've had advantages, my story is important for many different reasons.

First of all, remember to look at the complete picture. Over and over again, my challenges and my testing results have created barriers. My parents could have simply accepted that I had limited potential and not pushed forward. It's important for others to look at the objective testing results and to then see what I have managed to accomplish. Only then can they understand that such results do not make up the complete picture of potential. I believe this must be true for many other people; not just me. Please don't overlook potential.

Secondly, every achievement, no matter how small, should be applauded. I never understood the depth of my challenges. Looking back, it seems to me like this worked to my benefit. Instead of feeling negative about myself, I just kept working towards the next goal. The focus was on celebrating the accomplishments and not the fact that I was so far behind on the development spectrum.

Another important point concerns the fact that I have never been able to understand what people mean by my lack of social skills. If I could see my challenges on my own, I would adjust my behaviors. Thankfully, however, when something is pointed out to me in a very descriptive way, I can make a change in my behavior. For example, as

I mentioned earlier, I never understood in middle school that I was encroaching on people's personal space until my dad found a visual, and for me relatable, way to help me judge distance when I'm around people. Nothing like a force field to keep things appropriate! Another example relates to improving my social skills. I love to talk about the stories I am constructing in my mind, something I've done since I was a child. However, I now understand that if, instead of having a two-way conversation, someone only talked to me about what they were thinking, it would be challenging. Now, I try to work on asking people questions. It's not intuitive to me, but I can learn from examples.

As I pointed out, in addition to a supportive family, my life has been very blessed by people who went out of their way to give me an opportunity. This was not always easy. It takes time and effort for people to be flexible and include someone with challenges such as autism. My first Taido instructor, Sensei Uchida, is a great example of someone who wanted to give me an opportunity. It was a great gift. However, I was also held accountable. If I had not made an effort and showed my willingness to work, I would have not succeeded. But first I had to be given the chance.

Although I had the privilege of going to a school with a high teacher-to-student ratio, my parents and I still had to commit well beyond the traditional time to move me forward. What my parents did to assist me in college isn't normal, but I also had to do my part. If others studied one hour, we studied together for eight hours. Again, it was like training for a marathon. We put in the extra work and it paid off and my academic abilities kept improving. You have to do the time!

HIDDEN BLESSINGS

The first music teacher I had didn't work but the second one, Mrs. Richards, became a lifelong family friend. With great patience, she gave me a chance at the piano, but later helped spark a lifelong joy by teaching me to sing classical music. As this turned out to be the key to my college admission, it was a hidden blessing that the original music teacher was unwilling to deal with my challenges. Instead of worrying about what had gone wrong, my parents kept pushing towards those things that could work. Focusing on the negative things that were happening would have led to a very different outcome in my life.

Other aspects of my life may not seem important to others, but since they've helped shape who I am, either directly or indirectly, they've played a role in my success and therefore might provide helpful insight. One of things that I loved since before I can remember was watching television. Think about my testing results, and it's easy to see how playing a board game, working on a puzzle, or reading were just stressful for me. The TV provided a calm activity, and I could watch the same shows over and over again. As you know by now, I loved the *Power Rangers*, which I could totally relate to, especially during my martial arts classes. Any hero figure, like Batman or the Flash, were my favorite, and I loved cartoons too. My parents worried about "too much TV" but I maintain that my brain needed the repetition to learn to speak and relate.

Playing video games was also something I enjoyed, which I find interesting considering my lack of motor skills and difficulty in making quick, complex moves. My parents said that they were always concerned that too much time spent playing video games would hurt my development in other areas. Instead, they began to see how my reflexes and accuracy were improving while playing the games, which represented steps forward for me. Every time I started playing a new video game, I would be terrible at it, but over time would pick up speed and accuracy, which was very encouraging to my parents. They saw first-hand that I could improve with time and practice, and that became the approach they took with all of my challenges. With one goal at a time, I would achieve it and then set a new one.

FILE IT AWAY...ONE STEP AT A TIME

There's no doubt that I have the ability to learn; just not in a traditional way. It may be that others with autism share some of my traits as a strong visual learner. My challenge early in life was not being able to process auditory information at all, which set me on a path filled with even more obstacles to overcome. The example I use now to describe my brain is one of an empty file box that must gather and store information. My brain inserts information into different catalogues that I can pull from as needed. Over time, the file box becomes filled with many options, which make my responses more accurate than they were at one time. For example, my file box now contains duplicate definitions for the same word. When I was five years old, this was not the case. I didn't have enough exposure to information to fill all the empty file boxes in my head. This is why someone with autism may give an answer that seems like just a memorized statement. As the occupational therapist noted, I was unable to move to a new activity without more coaching and planning. But the more in the file box, the less stressful I am because I have information to help me with a new situation. My file-box-type brain also explains my lack of automated understanding of social situations. But just like with facts and figures, social situations can be catalogued over time, which helps people with autism improve their response over time.

Instead of focusing on what caused my autism and learning disabilities, finding next steps for my development has been a constant goal. With any list of problems, no matter if it's long or short, it's important not to feel overwhelmed and hopeless in the face of so many things that need attention. I used this technique in both college and graduate school. When I received the syllabus for a class, it was often very daunting. My parents taught me to focus only on what was due next and not become overwhelmed about the entire class. That same type of thought process works for all aspects of my personal life. What is the next important thing for me to work on? Obviously, my parents adopted this same approach about me: If they looked at everything I needed to accomplish to become self-sufficient in life, it would have been too overwhelming.

GLORIOUS GOALS

Change does not just occur. You have to form and harbor goals that make you challenge yourself to be better. While I had been achieving goals my entire life, the importance of this became even more obvious to me when I finished college. I felt very lost. School had been prescriptive so I always knew what I had to accomplish. Now I've managed to learn to think of and define where I'm trying to go next in my life. No goal is too small because every change makes a big difference. I also know that not everything I want to do will work out, but simply reaching for new goals is a lifelong pursuit.

When I was young, my parents and teachers set the goals. Now, it's up to me to decide what my next goals are. One of my passions is sharing the stories that have always been in my head. When I was young, I was unable to verbalize more than one sentence. Now, I work on writing my stories. As simple as this is for others, my brain had and still has difficulty completing this activity, but I keep pushing forward and now have managed to write several things.

No two people have the same challenges. However, the sheer number of problems that I have overcome demonstrates that simply focusing on an area that needs improvement can lead to a success-ful outcome in the long run. It's similar to someone training for a marathon. The ability to run a complete marathon doesn't happen overnight. Even with practice, some won't be as good as others, but eventually they're at least able to compete in the race.

GIVE AUTISM A CHANCE TO CHANGE

When I learned about my autism diagnosis, it was hard for me to comprehend the level of challenges I had faced. It was not how I saw myself. But it was so important for me to understand my deficits as I entered college so that I could share my needs with my professors. However, I wanted people to see that I was basically just like every-one else. The word "autism" has a stigma that many other disabilities don't. When I was initially diagnosed, my mom would encourage people to just give me a chance. She would say that autism would become the new "Helen Keller" story. No one thought that a blind, deaf and mute person had the same abilities as someone else. In the early 90s, when I was diagnosed, autism was viewed as a hopeless situation. It's a little better today, but there is no doubt that such a diagnosis limits the way others view that person's abilities. And yet, there are many people with autism who are simply brilliant, and others who have many, varied talents. I truly hoping my story changes the way people with autism and other disabilities are viewed.

Without the documentation of my testing, I would have never understood why others questioned my potential. When I read the results, it's not how I saw myself. Likewise, when I wasn't communicating, either in a social situation or during testing, I thought I was acting just like other children my age. This is a very important point to consider when dealing with others with autism. I'm sure I am not the only one who had a different view of his or her abilities. If someone doesn't speak, it doesn't necessarily mean that they're not processing what is happening around them. I am so grateful that my parents saw my potential in spite of it all.

As I have shared my story at different events, parents and family members of those with autism have asked me for advice. Initially, I couldn't believe that anyone would be asking me what I "thought!" After giving it some consideration, I realized that encouraging others not to give up on their child's potential is so important. No one can predict what another person can accomplish in life. It's so very complex. The ability to do something is not as important as the will to do it. You can possess all the ability in the world and accomplish nothing.

Testing is important because it helps define any areas of weakness so someone can work to improve. However, as seen in my situation, testing can also lead to an inaccurate prognosis of potential. My mom has described to me the feeling of hopelessness each time my testing was reviewed. Many times, she would find herself questioning her optimistic outlook on my potential. My dad always told her I would be fine.

Another significant takeaway from my story concerns the attempt to predict a child's future based on timing and development. No matter what gains I would make, I continued to be so far behind the development of other children, my positive strides getting trampled by their continued pace. Measuring developmental milestones for children does not predict long-term outcomes. No one can be compared to another person. In my situation, I have become a more responsible, capable adult than some who grew up hitting all the key milestones at just the right time.

I have always had the same hopes and dreams as others. It just may not have been obvious. When Sensei said, "Never give up and do your best," he was giving me the roadmap to find my true potential.

Acknowledgements

As I write this acknowledgement, I realize that this book would not exist without the love, support, and encouragement of so many people.

My parents, brother, sister-in-law and large extended family (aunts, uncles, cousins and nannies) deserve credit for always being there for me. It's just the way our family is with each other. This is definitely an advantage I have had. A special thanks to my mom for helping me with this book, and to my uncle, John Haigwood, who is responsible for the photos of me on the book cover.

It's the people outside my family who really deserve special recognition. Unlike so many who were unwilling to give me an opportunity, the following people took a risk and changed my life trajectory: Mrs. Jan Bowyer, my kindergarten teacher, who was willing to allow me in her class when others would not; Mill Springs Academy, for my twelve-year journey with faculty and staff, who encouraged me to keep trying; Mrs. Francesca' Richards, a former opera singer, who helped me find my talent and is like a grandmother to me; Dr. Kevin Hibbard, dean of the Music program at University of West Georgia, who saw my singing talent instead of my disability; Reinhardt University Masters of Business Administration faculty, who treated me just like the other students; Ms. Valerie Wheat, Center for Autism Studies, Jacksonville State University, who gave me my first opportunity to be the keynote speaker at their major autism conference; U.S. Taido Karate Black Belts, a group of diverse individuals, who share a common bond of kindness and respect for each other; Mr. Mitsuaki Uchida, now the head instructor at Taido, who has been a fierce supporter of me from the time I was six years old; and Mr. Brendan Dumont, an assistant instructor at Taido, who became one of my first friends and mentor.

Finally, I dedicate the book with more gratitude and admiration than I can describe to:

Mr. Mitsunobu Uchida, founder and President of U.S. Taido Association, Inc., who allowed me to join his martial arts program when I was six years old. He has had a profound effect on many lives because of his ability to accept all individuals as they are. He expects people to give their best effort and to never give up. In more ways than anyone can image, Taido has played a significant role in my success. It is a place where I belong.

References

Interviews by Author

Brendan Dumont. Interview by phone. February 16, 2017.

Dr. Kevin Hibbard. Interview by phone. February 1, 2017.

Dr. Katherine Hyatt. Interview by phone. February 8, 2017.

Robert Moore. Interview by phone. February 21, 2017.

Mitsuaki Uchida. Interview by phone. February 9, 2017.

Publications

Bahrami F., Movahedi A., Marandi SM, and Sorensen C. "The Effect of Karate Techniques

Training on Communication Deficit of Children with Autism Spectrum Disorders."

Journal of Autism and Developmental Disorders. March 2016.

Beery, Keith E., Norman A. Buktenica, and Natasha A. Beery. *Beery-Buktenica*

Developmental Test of Visual-Motor Integration, Sixth Edition, The (BEERY™ VMI).

New York, New York: Pearson, 2010.

Carrow-Woolfolk, Elizabeth. *Carrow Auditory-Visual Abilities Test.* Hingham, Mass: Teaching

Resources Corp., 1981.

Cohen, Morris J. *Children's Memory Scale.* New York, New York: Pearson, 1997.

The Critical Thinking Co. "Test Prep Guide for the Wechsler Preschool and Primary Scale of

Intelligence™." February 8, 2017.

http://www.criticalthinking.com/articles/test-preparation-practice-for-wppsi-assessment

Duckworth, Angela. *Grit: The Power of Passion and Perserverance.* New York, New York:

Scribner, First Edition, 2016.

Folio, Rhonda M. and Rebecca R. Fewell. Peabody Developmental Motor Scales, Second

Edition. New York, New York: Pearson, 2000.

Grant, David A. and Esta A. Berg. *Wisconsin Card Sorting Test.* Torrance, California: WPS, 1981.

Milone, Michael N. and Zaner-Bloser. *A Common Approach to Learning: the Swassing-Barbe Modality Index.* Columbus, Ohio: Zaner-Bloser, 1979.

Morris, Betty, Lisa Munoz and Patricia Neering. "Overcoming Dyslexia." *Fortune.* May 13, 2002.

Rindfleisch, Terry. "UW-L Study: Martial Arts Benefit Autistic Kids." *La Crosse Tribune.* December 15, 2010.

Roid, Gale PhD, Lucy J. Miller, PhD, et al. *Leiter International Performance Scale, Third Edition*. Torrance, California: WPS, 2013.

Woodcock-Johnson Test Series, Fourth Edition. New York, New York: Houghton Mifflin Harcourt.

Websites

American Music Therapy Association. http://www.musictherapy.org.

Dolch Sight Words. http://www.sightwords.com/sight-words/dolch/.

Marcus Autism Center. http://www.marcus.org.

Mill Springs Academy. https://www.millsprings.org.

National Institute of Neurological Disorders and Stroke. "Developmental Dyspraxia Information

Page." https://www.ninds.nih.gov/disorders/all-disorders/developmental-dyspraxia-information-page.

National Institute on Deafness and Other Communication Disorders. https://www.nidcd.nih.gov.

Endnotes

Chapter 1: A Doubtful Future
[1] Testing Report from 3/8/92 by Children's Speech and Hearing Services
[2] Language Pathology Diagnostic Services, Testing Dates June 15, 16,17, 1992
[3] According to Michael's mother, when he was diagnosed, the description of PDD's was as follows: "The pervasive developmental disorders (PDDs) are characterized by patterns of deviance and delay in social-communicative development in the first years of life, which are associated with restricted patterns of interest or behaviour." *International Classification of Diseases: Diagnostic Criteria for Research* (Tenth Edition). Geneva, World Health Organization (1992)

"I don't think it was a clinical error, but more a characterization error," Joane Goodroe explains. "No matter the reason, it was a tremendous gift for me to see the word 'delay.'"

[4] The Adaptive Learning Center, Testing Date July 16, 1992

Chapter 2: Looking for Any Open Door
[5] Speech Language Pathology and Audiology Clinic, Progress Report, January 1993
[6] Speech Language Pathology and Audiology Clinic, Progress Report, May, 1993

[7]   Speech Language Pathology and Audiology Clinic, Progress Report, October 1993

[8]   The Carrow Auditory Visual Abilities Test, October 1993

[9]   Test of Language Competence (Expanded Edition), November 1993

[10]   Occupational Therapy Report, November 1993

[11]   The following tests were performed at The Adaptive Learning Center, January 1994, which identified very specific strengths and weaknesses:

1. **Motor-Free Visual Perception: This test evaluated my ability to visually perceive and discriminate form and space without involving motor coordination. Results show that I was within the normal range for my age. This is why I learned best with visual information as opposed to auditory information.**

2. **Somatosensory: Five tests were used to assess areas of tactile, muscle, and joint perception, and these tests are administered without visual cues. I did well on tactile perception but at times, showed defensive signs with avoidance behavior. I was unable to hold a form in my hand and then identify the correct shape on a chart. My scores on this test were very low. This meant that I was not able to translate what I felt I was holding without actually seeing it.**

3. **Praxis is the ability to plan and carry out skilled movements. It refers to new or complex motor tasks which are not automatic in nature. An example is learning to tie shoes, which requires motor planning, attention, practice, and concentration. Once something is learned, it no longer requires motor planning, attention, practice, and concentration. There were several tests to evaluate different types of praxis:**

   • **Praxis on verbal command is the ability to assume certain body positions in response to verbal directions. This was the area where I had the greatest difficulty and showed the lowest score on the testing.**

- **Postural Praxis is done by asking the person to follow certain positions with a visual model with no verbal directions. I scored in the average range for this area which supported that my greatest difficulty seemed to be in processing the auditory information rather than the motoric skill required to carry out the action.**
- **One of the tests was for me to copy simple designs; I was below average, which indicates difficulty with two-dimensional visuospatial skills. In addition, I had a great deal of trouble and did not intuitively know to stop at the end of a line and realign the pen to draw something else. This is still a challenge for me today.**
- **Another test involved three-dimensional visual space management, which required me to duplicate a block structure using a model. Once again, my score was below average. I was unable to perceive the spatial orientation of the blocks and unable to judge how sizes would fit together. At six years old, just a simple puzzle that a two-year-old could have completed was impossible for me.**
- **I was also asked to imitate tongue, lip, and jaw movements. Again, I was below average for my age. Tests for Bilateral Motor Coordination, Standing, Walking Balance, and Motor Accuracy all showed below average scores.**

[12] The Adaptive Learning Center, January 1994
[13] www.ninds.nih.gov/Disorders/All-Disorders/Developmental-Dyspraxia-Information-Page
[14] The Adaptive Learning Center, January 1994
[15] The Adaptive Learning Center, January 1994
[16] Report from The Marcus Center, February, 1994
[17] Speech Language Pathology and Audiology Clinic, Wechsler Preschool and Primary Scale of Intelligence Testing; Report Date February, 1994

[18] Speech Language Pathology and Audiology Clinic, Wechsler Preschool and Primary Scale of Intelligence Testing; Report Date February, 1994

[19] Speech Language Pathology and Audiology Clinic, Progress Report June, 1994

[20] Speech Language Pathology and Audiology Clinic, Progress Report June, 1994

[21] Speech Language Pathology and Audiology Clinic, Progress Report June, 1994

Chapter 3: Consistently Earns Fabulous Friday

[22] Swassing-Barbe Modality Index, September 1994

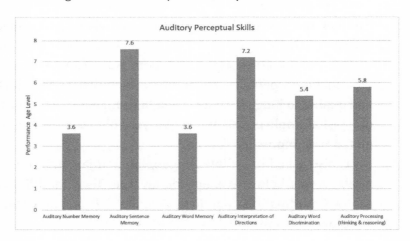

Chapter 4: Lost in Autistic Translation

[23] Here's an example of an essay I wrote at the end of third grade:

> I got my puppy last year and I name my dog Zeo and I got the cat before I was born. My puppy is cute she is my puppy and I love her I like my cat to I love them. I like my Brother.

Sentence structure and thought process were significantly lacking, but I had made progress compared to where I had been.

[24] The following were listed as my consistent strengths.

1. Ignores other inappropriate behavior.
2. Waits turn and listens while another person is talking.

126

3. Follows directions.
4. Sits in place with rocking, fidgeting, or touching others.
5. Uses courtesy words.
6. Stays on subject.
7. Identifies own feelings.
8. Verbalizes positive comments.
9. Shows empathy for other people.
10. Understands emotion represented various "feeling" words.
11. Asks questions related to the subject.
12. Feels free to share own personal experience with others.
13. Displays improved understanding of cause and effect relationship, academic and social relationships.

25 Sixth Grade progress report summaries:

Reading: Michael has had a successful semester. He is a wonderful student and is a pleasure to teach. Keep it up. Areas noted as inconsistent performance: Understands sound/symbol relationship; remembers details; keeps place while reading; makes inferences; reads a variety of genres

Language Arts: Michal has shown growth in his writing this semester. Using computer to help with spelling. Low scoring areas: spelling, does not understand parts of speech; does not write complete paragraphs, does not write in a variety of styles.

Math: An excellent motivated student. Michael's assignments are well-done and completed on time. I am bursting with pride at his progress. What a wonderful math student. Ready for next level. Low scoring areas: Applies math skills to word problems/life skills.

Science: Michael is wonderful. He seems to enjoy science and is a pleasure to teach. Areas of challenge: Relates concepts/facts to lab work, relates demonstrations to classwork; ability to draw conclusions.

Social Studies: Michael gives 100% of his effort on all activities but he is challenged in offering information spontaneously, retaining some facts.

Values: Michael has contributed positively in class. He is getting better at verbalizing his feelings.

Computer: Michael makes a great effort in classes. Areas needing improvement: Inadequate eye-hand coordination; word processing; researching topics; completing work on time; relating concept to projects.

PE: Over the years, Michael has improved in his efforts. He is involved and interested. He seems to enjoy all the different activities. He is very happy and sings during activities. I love his humor and positive nature.

Chapter 5: Fast Track Backwards
[26] Psychological Evaluation for Educational Planning, Dates of Evaluation: October 31st, November 7th, 13th, 28th and December 15th, 2001

The psychologist gave the following summary from her interactions with me:

Michael was somewhat large for his age, which made him appear older than 14 years old. Michael easily established and maintained a good rapport with the examiner. He tended to relate in a mature manner, such as shaking the examiner's hand and appearing confident. However, his social affect was somewhat off and his vocal tone quality and affect were flat. Although he was talkative, he had difficulty engaging in the reciprocity or give and take required for conversation. He tended to hold forth rather than converse. He did not modulate the volume of his voice for the setting, speaking rather loudly. Michael cooperated with all tasks presented. However, when the tasks became more difficult and he became frustrated, he would attempt to stop an activity with somatic complaints, stating that he did not feel good or that his head hurt. He appeared easily frustrated. Throughout the one-on-one evaluation sessions, Michael appeared attentive and

his activity level was normal. He tended to respond impulsively. He frequently attempted to start an activity before he knew what he was to do. On pencil and paper tasks, he consistently used his right hand. His pencil grasp was awkward and his control of the pencil was weak.

27   In addition, my parents reported my strengths as "his caring and kindness to others, his level of responsibility, his memorization skills and his self-confidence. He is very close to his family and does not feel the need for friends outside of the family. Michael's thinking tends to be concrete and rigid. He can become over focused on something and somewhat obsessive. He is a picky eater and will only eat certain foods and textures. He just recently started eating some meats. Michael enjoys karate and video games."

28   Psychological Evaluation for Educational Planning, Dates of Evaluation: October 31st, November 7th, 13th, 28th and December 15th, 2001

This graph from the Verbal Scale subset of the Wechsler Intelligence Scale demonstrates that there was only one area, Information, in which I scored within the average range. I scored below average in all other categories.

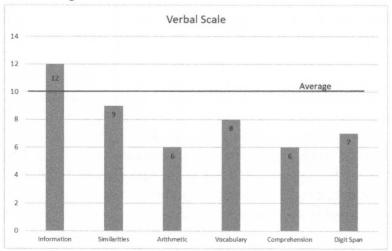

29

Psychological Evaluation for Educational Planning, Dates of Evaluation: October 31st, November 7th, 13th, 28th and December 15th, 2001

The second group of subsets was called Performance Scale: Picture Completion, Coding, Picture Arrangement, Block Design, Object Assembly, and Symbol Search. Note the enormous variation in this group with Picture Arrangement being a strength and Coding falling at the very low end of the scale.

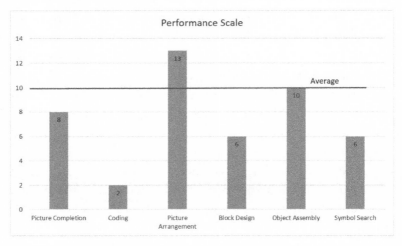

30

Psychological Evaluation for Educational Planning, Dates of Evaluation: October 31st, November 7th, 13th, 28th and December 15th, 2001

Index scores were used in place of IQ scores. An index is considered in the average range when scores fall between 90 and 109. The areas of Verbal Comprehension and Perceptual Organization fall in the low-average levels. The percentile performance is 32nd and 39th. In comparison to other testing, this was an improvement. Freedom from Distractibility, at the 10th percentile, was below average. My Processing Speed was extremely low, a 70, which put me in the 2nd percentile. These last two areas showed significant deficits in performance.

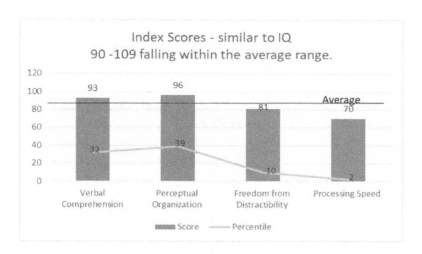

Index Scores - similar to IQ
90 -109 falling within the average range.

Psychological Evaluation for Educational Planning, Dates of Evaluation: October 31st, November 7th, 13th, 28th and December 15th, 2001

My visual processing was assessed using both the Visual Closure and Spatial Relations subtests of the WJ-R COG. On the Visual Closure test, I was asked to identify a picture from an incomplete presentation. I scored a standard score of 79, which was the 8th percentile, with an age equivalent of 8 years and 3 months. This was considered borderline. Spatial Relations tested my ability to identify parts that make up a whole figure. My score of 84 was in the 15th percentile with an age equivalent of 8 years, which was the low average range. Overall, I performed poorly on this part of the testing.

Psychological Evaluation for Educational Planning, Dates of Evaluation: October 31st, November 7th, 13th, 28th and December 15th, 2001

Visual motor skills were evaluated using the Beery Developmental Test of Visual-Motor Integration and Rey Complex Figure. I obtained a standard score of 83, which was in the 13th percentile and had an age equivalent of 9 years 6 months which was within the low average range. It was noted that I had particular difficulty "integrating the parts of the design into a whole."

[33] Psychological Evaluation for Educational Planning, Dates of Evaluation: October 31st, November 7th, 13th, 28th and December 15th, 2001

Verbal and visual memory, including both immediate and delayed, were assessed utilizing the Children's Memory Scale (CMS). My general memory score was 81, 10th percentile, which was low average. Visual memory fell within the average and low average ranges and was somewhat stronger than my low average verbal memory. I also scored in the low average range on subtests most sensitive to attention and concentration, which measured working memory (the ability to hold information in memory long enough to perform an operation).

The following chart is derived from the Children's Memory Score. A score of 100 is considered average. My ability in the Learning category, with a score of 109 in the 73rd percentile, fell within the average range and was the one positive note from this entire test.

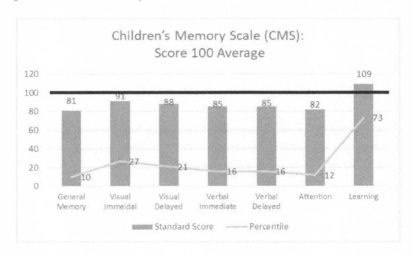

³⁴ The psychologist who performed the testing in October attended one of my classes in late March 2002. I did not know she was coming, but I recognized her right away. This is her documentation of her class observation:

March 25, 2002: Michael was observed in his GA History class at MSA. The class consisted of six students, including Michael. Michael sat at a three-sided carrel while some of the other students sat together at the tables. While it was intended that the examiner would observe the class anonymously, Michael immediately jumped up, shook hands with the examiner and introduced her to the class, identifying her as "his psychologist." He did not appear to have any concerns or self-consciousness of being observed.

> In the beginning of the class, Michael activity participated, raising his hand and answering questions. The class was reviewing a study sheet that had been assigned as homework. Michael had clearly completed the assignment correctly. While other students had their textbooks open following along and were taking notes on their assignment sheet and on laptop computers, Michael's book was closed and the computer was stored in its carrying case. As the class progressed, Michael appeared to tune out. However, he responded appropriately when called upon by the teacher. He later opened both his textbook and his computer.

> Michael's participation in an informal class discussion was borderline appropriate. His addition to the discussion was rather tangential and did not provoke a response by the other students. During a break time, he ran an errand for the teacher to get some construction paper for the class. He came back after a few minutes to ask how much paper was needed. Later, another student returned with the paper.

> Michael got back to work quickly after the break, even before all of the other students had returned and before the teacher instructed

the class to get to work. The assignment was a writing exercise. Michael worked on his laptop computer and was observed to use the spell-check program appropriately. As he was working on the exercise, he stated, "I am better at explaining than writing."

Michael's behavior and class participation during the observed class was appropriate. He knew the material and had accurately completed his homework assignment. His attention seemed to waver some during the class. However, he continued to respond appropriately and he did not disturb other students. His social interaction with his classmates was minimal.

Book Review
- was it well-
  written (concise)
- Themes.

- Why someone
  would read
  this.

- Did I connect
  with the book
  & my own
  experience with
  autism.

<u>Easy to Read</u>

Testing is a
THEME. So
is hope and
self-esteem.
Parent advocacy

- Taido
- 3 key influence → school, martial arts & music
- Michael's strengths pg. 88

CPSIA information can be obtained
at www.ICGtesting.com
Printed in the USA
BVHW030154160223
658577BV00007B/718

9 781478 797821